Horseback Riding Trails
of
Southern California

Volume II

Here's what the experts said about *Volume 1* of the series:

"Everything imaginable is noted about a trail, from the open hours or seasons to access to hitching rails, water for both horses and people, and restrooms, even the gain in elevation on a given stretch of the route."
Western Horseman

———◆———

"I have just received a copy of your very helpful and inspiring trail book, and it's such a handy size, too."
Liz Grogan, North American Trail Ride Conference member

———◆———

"Great book! I love mine."
Eleanor Frazier, chairman of the Trail Riders Award Program,
California State Horsemen's Association, Region II

———◆———

"The author has created a rich guide...The information ranges from poetic descriptions of spring wildflower displays to warnings about big trucks and trailers that could get permanently stuck in a small parking area...There's a trail for everyone in this small book, which fits easily in a saddlebag."
Carol Storke, The Santa Barbara Independent

———◆———

"You've done a marvelous job!"
Gwen Allen, past president of Equestrian Trails, Inc.

———◆———

"I liked the amount of time Mouchet spent on safety tips, a first-aid and supply list, etc. Basically, Mouchet gives you a list of trails to try and the information to let you know if that trail is doable for you."
Valerie Zera, Antelope Valley Press

"We've needed this book for years!"
Holly Carson, publisher *Equestrian Trails* magazine

———◆———

"Mouchet's extensive research and love of the subject are evident in every entry…[Horseback Riding Trails of Southern California] tells you everything you need to know before you hitch up your trailer."
Margo Murman, livestock manager of Leonis Adobe Museum

———◆———

"I'm very impressed."
Nola Michel, past president of Backcountry Horsemen, San Diego Unit

———◆———

"You should really be proud of this book. It's absolutely superior."
Connie Burns, publisher *Horsin' Around* magazine

———◆———

"We ordered a dozen books before Christmas and they're all gone."
Norco Ranch Outfitters

———◆———

"I just got my copy and love it."
Theresa Burger, administrator of the on-line Horse Trails home page

———◆———

"Paulette Mouchet has provided what all trail riders love most—the opportunity to seek the mystery and adventure of new paths."
Julie Suhr, American Endurance Ride Conference Hall of Fame rider

———◆———

"It's great! An essential step toward making trails truly accessible."
Linda Palmer, past president of the Santa Monica Mountains Trails Council

HORSEBACK RIDING TRAILS
OF
SOUTHERN CALIFORNIA

VOLUME II

BY
PAULETTE MOUCHET

CROWN VALLEY PRESS
P.O. BOX 336
ACTON, CA 93510-0336
(805) 269-1525

IMPORTANT LEGAL NOTICE AND DISCLAIMER

Horseback riding is a potentially dangerous sport, and the rider or user of this book accepts a number of risks. While substantial effort has been made to provide accurate information, this guidebook may inadvertently contain errors and omissions. The maps in this book are for locator reference only. They are not to be used for navigation and are intended to complement large-scale topo maps. Your mileages may vary from those given in this book.

The author, contributors, publisher, and distributors accept no liability for any errors or omissions in this book, or for any injuries or losses incurred from using this book.

Copyright © 1996 Paulette Mouchet

Photos by George Mouchet except as noted.
Front cover photo: Cachuma Lake Equestrian Trail.
Back cover photos: top, Upper Oso Campground; middle, Frank G. Bonelli Regional County Park; bottom, Red Box.

Cover and interior design: Patricia de Sota, Nevada City CA.
Drawings by Laurie Ebert-Berger, Littlerock CA.

First Printing 1996.

ISBN 0-9647945-1-9

Library of Congress Catalog Card Number 95-92581

Library of Congress Cataloging-in-Publication Data
Mouchet, Paulette
    Horseback Riding Trails of Southern California Volume II/Paulette Mouchet.
    v. :ill. ; 160 p.; 21.6 cm.
    Includes bibliographical references and index.
    ISBN 0-9647945-1-9
    1. Trails — California — Guide-books. 2. California, Southern — Description and travel — Guide-books. 3. California — Description and travel — 1981- — Guide-books. 4. Horses — Miscellanea. 5. Horse sports. I. Title

979.40T M924 1996   95-92581
                                                         CIP

ACKNOWLEDGMENTS

As with any book of this nature, turning the dream into reality takes more than jeans in the saddle and fingers at the computer keyboard. Without the ideas, suggestions, enthusiasm, and support of the wonderful folks I met along the trail, I would have given up long ago and missed out on a great adventure in doing so.

I'd like to thank my husband who has championed my writing from the beginning. After two books, he is *still* my faithful riding companion, chauffeur, computer guru, camera wizard, and all-around the most wonderful man a woman could have.

Special thanks again to my adopted mother, Pat, for her generosity and for encouraging me to follow my dreams.

Thanks to Jennifer and Rick Fuller for their enthusiasm, for exploring new trails, and for sharing some great camping meals.

Thanks to Laurie Ebert-Berger for the gorgeous pen and ink drawings and her undying friendship.

Thanks to Joan Phelan, Betty Swift, and Barbara C. Zimmerman for taking the time and energy to contribute trails to this volume. Thanks also to Margaret Brenner for sharing the Phantom Trail and her knowledge of the Malibu Creek area. And thanks to the many folks I've met via phone and in person who have suggested new trails for me to check out. Some of them are here and some will be in *Volume III*.

Thanks to Wayne Marteney, DVM, for squeezing time out of his busy schedule to review the "First-Aid Kit." Thanks to Sharon at PeopleSpeak for her eagle eye editing, great humor, and marketing savvy. Thanks to Holly Carson, editor of the *Equestrian Trails* magazine, for all her encouragement, support, and advice.

Finally, thanks to our four-footed friends, Sam and Centella, who faithfully carried my husband and me on the many miles of trails we explored. And I've been admonished by several friends for not mentioning that they are Peruvian Pasos.

ABOUT THE AUTHOR

Paulette Mouchet has owned horses for more than twenty-five years and enjoys riding and exploring new trails with her husband. She is a member of Equestrian Trails, Inc.; Backcountry Horsemen of California; the Santa Monica Mountains Trails Council; the Antelope Valley Trails, Recreation, and Environmental Council; and the Southern California Peruvian Paso Horse Club. She writes both fiction and nonfiction, and her work has been published in magazines and newspapers.

TABLE OF CONTENTS

TRAILS BY COUNTY

TRAILS BY REGION/CITY

LIST OF MAPS

LIST OF DRAWINGS
By Laurie Ebert-Berger

PREFACE

Thank you for purchasing Volume II of *Horseback Riding Trails of Southern California.*

When my husband and I bought our first horse trailer, we could not find a practical guide to riding trails. Being new to trailering, we didn't want to hook up and drive someplace when we didn't know exactly where that "someplace" was, or if there would be trailer parking when we got there, or if our horses could handle the trails. As we collected information for ourselves, it seemed obvious and appropriate that we should make it available to anyone who wanted to experience new trails. Thus, *Horseback Riding Trails of Southern California,* the series, was born. *Volume I,* published in late 1995, became a runaway success—a clear indicator of the need for such a book. I think you'll agree that *Volume II* meets the standard of excellence established in *Volume I.*

My continuing goal is to provide accurate directions and detailed information about facilities so that you can get to a location, park, and enjoy exploring the trails yourself. Many sites have overnight facilities and I have indicated them. Horseback riding is an activity that the entire family can enjoy, and I hope you have as much fun as my husband and I did.

From the time I began this project until now, trail conditions may have changed, new trails may have been developed, and others may have been lost due to neglect. If you have comments or suggestions, or would like to contribute to the series, please write to me in care of Crown Valley Press. I would like to hear from you.

Good riding!

SAFETY FIRST

Safety Tips

Plan ahead. Keep your cool. Carry first-aid supplies.

Newcomers and seasoned riders alike should be aware that horseback riding can be a dangerous sport. Accidents can happen in the blink of an eye, sometimes in remote locations. The goal of this book is for you and your horse to have an enjoyable ride. Don't let that be ruined by an avoidable mishap. Please take a few minutes to read the following safety tips.

- Condition yourself and your horse. Too many accidents occur because the horse and/or rider just aren't up to the job. A tired horse may stumble and throw the rider. A tired rider may take unnecessary risks.

- Check and maintain your equipment. This includes your trailer as well as your tack. Follow your trailer manufacturer's maintenance schedule for wheel bearings and brakes.

- Don't ride alone. If you or your horse is hurt, your buddy can go for help.

- Carry a halter, pocket knife, wire cutters, and water. See page 143 for a list of general supplies to bring.

- Wear protective clothing. Consider protective head gear. Hard hats are available in western hat styles. See page 150 for a list of manufacturers.

- Observe good trail manners. See page 23 for guidelines. Don't crowd each other, especially going up and down hills, and don't race.

- Carry a basic first-aid kit for both you and your horse. See pages 145–146 for a suggested first-aid kit. Check your kit every 6 months and replace items that are expired or depleted.

- Know your limits and stick to them. Don't let others pressure you into riding farther or faster than you or your horse are conditioned for.

A CB radio or cellular phone in your towing vehicle may be helpful, and you might consider taking a CPR and basic first-aid course. For classes in your area, contact your local Red Cross.

Ultimately, be prepared. Knowledge of first aid and basic safety rules will give you self-confidence and enable you to more thoroughly enjoy your ride.

Mountain Lions

Many of the trails listed in this guide traverse mountain lion country. To see a lion in its native habitat can be a thrilling part of your ride. However, mountain lions, also known as cougars, panthers, or pumas, are wild predators and deserve your utmost respect. An adult male averages 6 feet long and can weigh 165 pounds. The head is relatively small with a black spot above each eye, the feet oversized, and the tail thick and nearly as long as the body. With growing urban expansion into wildlife habitat, an increased number of human/lion encounters have been reported. Always stay alert when riding. You are a visitor in their territory.

If you see a mountain lion:

* Do not approach.
* Make yourself look as big as possible and slowly back away.
* Do not run or make sudden moves.
* Do not dismount or crouch down.
* Report any sightings to the appropriate agency.
* Keep your dog on a leash. Better yet, leave him home.

Rattlesnakes

Rattlesnakes are a common southern California inhabitant ranging from the coast to the higher mountain elevations. Of the six species found, the Western rattlesnake (*Crotalus viridis*) is the most widespread. While any rattlesnake bite is serious, the Mojave rattler (*C. scutulatus*) bite is the most deadly. Your best defense against a snakebite is to stay alert and give a wide berth to any snake you encounter. Most snakes will leave you alone if you give them the chance.

According to Glenn R. Stewart, Ph.D., bites from most rattlesnakes are not a life or death matter. Between 20 and 30 percent of rattlesnake bites introduce no venom at all, and most bites introduce venom only into the subcutaneous tissue.

The action of venom includes direct destruction of tissues and blood vessels, which causes much swelling and pain at the site of the bite. Venom of the Mojave rattlesnake impairs nerve and neuromuscular function, and the bite produces little swelling or pain.

Early symptoms of mild to moderate envenomation from most rattle-snake bites include mild swelling or discoloration and mild to moderate pain at the site of the bite. These symptoms are often accompanied by tingling, rapid pulse, weakness, dimness of vision, nausea, vomiting, and shortness of breath.

Symptoms of severe envenomation include rapid swelling and numbness followed by intense pain at the site of the bite. Other symptoms include pinpoint pupils, twitching, slurred speech, shock, convulsions, paralysis, unconsciousness, and failure of breathing and pulse.

Snake Identification

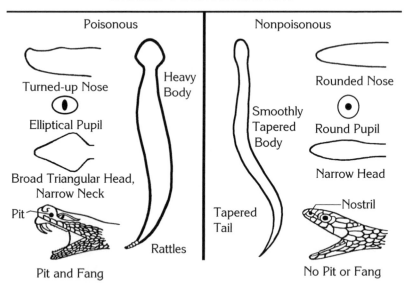

The definitive treatment is antivenin (purified serum, usually from horses, containing antibodies to neutralize the venom components). If antivenin is administered within 60 minutes of the bite, the chances of death from most bites are quite small. A victim in a truly remote area (more than 1 hour from medical treatment) may benefit from the use of powerful suction (e.g., the "Sawyer Extractor") at the bite site. Antivenin can be administered in the field by untrained persons. You may want to consult with your family physician regarding the use of antivenin and/or the Sawyer Extractor.

If you are bitten:

- Remain calm.
- Remove rings, bracelets, watchbands, etc., from all extremities.
- Immobilize the bitten part with a sling or splint.
- Keep bitten part below heart level and minimize physical activity.
- Seek medical treatment as soon as possible.
- Have your riding partner try to capture and kill the snake so it may be presented for positive identification when you receive medical treatment.

Ticks

With Lyme disease on the rise in California and the nation, you should take precautions against ticks, the most common known vector of the disease. Caused by the corkscrew-shaped bacteria *Borrelia burgdorferi*, Lyme disease affects both humans and animals.

Some signs of the disease in humans:

- Rash with large, distinctive circular lesions first seen around the area of the bite (only 50–60 percent of patients have this rash); rash may come and go
- Malaise
- Fever
- Muscle aches
- Swollen lymph glands

This list is not complete. Consult your physician for more information.

Deer ticks are the most common carrier of Lyme disease. They are very small, approximately 1/16-inch wide, and orange-brown with a black spot near the head.

After any ride, check yourself thoroughly and immediately seek medical attention if you have been bitten and notice any of the symptoms listed. If not treated early, the disease can affect heart function and cause arthritis of the major joints.

Wear long sleeves and pants when riding, and use an insect repellent designed for ticks. Apply a tick-killing fly spray to your horse and routinely check all animals for ticks.

If you find an imbedded tick, touch it with a heated knife. The tick will "back out" allowing you to grab and squash it with tweezers or a hemostat. Thoroughly wash the bite area, your hands, and all removal equipment.

Poison Oak

For most people, an encounter with poison oak results in an inflamed, red, scaly, and extremely itchy rash that heals in approximately 2 to 3 weeks. Occasionally, a person is hyperallergic and will develop severe dermatitis and possibly anaphylactic shock if he or she does not receive immediate medical treatment. The rash is spread by scratching. Oral antihistamine and over-the-counter hydrocortisone cream will help control the itching. In more severe cases, oral steroids may be prescribed by your family doctor.

Take the time to recognize this plant in all its disguises, and then avoid it! Poison oak is widespread throughout the areas listed in this guide. Normally an erect shrub 4 to 8 feet tall, it sometimes twines along the trunks of trees. The leaves are bright green in the spring, turn orange or scarlet in the fall, and may drop off during the winter. In March and April you may see small, greenish-white flowers that become pea-sized white berries in the summer. The leaves are oval, lobed, approximately 2 inches long, and always come in threes.

Fire

Beginning in May, southern California enters its "fire season." The chaparral slows its growth and begins to dry out, the grass turns yellow, the humidity drops, and temperatures rise. Conditions intensify through June, July, and August. In the fall, they are compounded by hot, dry Santa Ana winds that blow in from the northeastern deserts. In the Angeles National Forest alone, more than one hundred fires are started by people each year. If you plan to ride during the "fire season," be aware of local fire danger and plan in advance your escape route if a fire erupts suddenly. Before you ride, check trail conditions and closures with the trail administering agency. Remember Smokey's motto: Only You Can Prevent Forest Fires.

If you see a fire:

* Return to your vehicle at once and leave the area.
* When in a safe place, dial 911 and report the location to local authorities.

Quicksand

Quicksand generally forms only under slow-moving or still water. To avoid riding into quicksand, stick to well-used trails and cross rivers and creeks where the water is moving quickly.

GUIDELINES FOR RIDING CONDUCT

✓ Before leaving your vehicle, ask yourself: Is there room for others to park, load, and unload?

✓ Do your part in keeping the trailhead clean and accessible to others. Bring a rake and shovel. On streets and paved parking lots, pick up your animal's manure. On trails and in dirt parking lots, break it up and scatter it.

✓ Greet everyone with a smile and friendly hello.

✓ Be of assistance when a need arises.

✓ Stay on the trail. Cutting across switchbacks causes erosion. Remove obstacles from trails whenever possible rather than riding around them.

✓ When meeting other trail users (including mountain bicyclists) on narrow trails, ask them to stand to the outside edge of the trail and continue talking (and not make any sudden movements) while you pass them. Since horses do not see well above them, it's helpful if other trail users can stand below the eye level of your horse.

✓ If your horse paws the ground, do not tie him to a tree. Use a "tree-saver" or other padding to prevent your rope from cutting into the bark and damaging the tree.

✓ Don't smoke while riding. Make absolutely sure your smoking material is extinguished and buried when through.

✓ Leave your dog at home.

Ocotillo
(Fouquieria splendens)

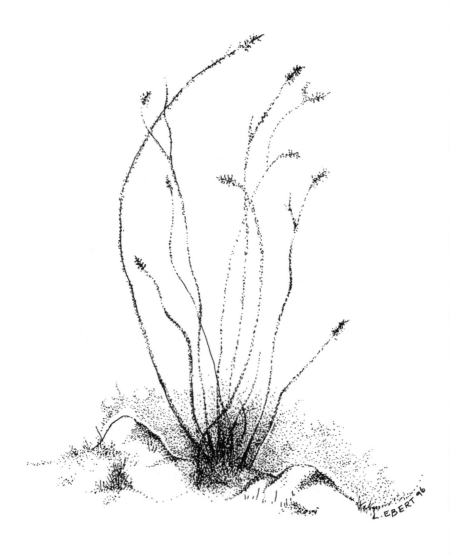

L. EBERT 96

TRAILERING TIPS:
Before You Go and On The Road

By John Lyons

(Reprinted with permission from *Ride!* magazine and
Maverick Advertising and Public Relations)

Having trailered my horse Zip more than a million miles over the past 20 years, I can tell you one thing for sure: It pays to plan ahead and know what's up the road before you begin each trip.

Throughout my travels across the country to horse shows, training clinics, symposiums, trail rides, and other events, I have encountered many odd, interesting, and dangerous situations. I've also seen problems that visitors to my Colorado ranch have dealt with while trailering their horse from across the United States and Canada—even those who have made the trip five or six times over the past 18 months.

Drawing on these experiences, I have developed some ideas on how to make trailering as easy and safe as possible for you and your horse: Here are a few:

Before you go: Always plan ahead. Try to familiarize yourself with the travel route before you leave, and identify good places to stay overnight—preferably locations with a motel for you and a clean stall or corral for your horse.

Before every trip, inspect your trailer to make sure it is in good working order. Pay special attention to the tires, brake lights, door latches, and other potential trouble spots. A worn out, rickety trailer is unsafe for everyone.

A couple of weeks before you leave on your trip, visit your veterinarian to get your horse's health papers in line. These documents are a "must" in most cases and should be properly maintained. Also, consider having your vet give your horse stress vaccine shots in preparation for the journey. These shots boost your horse's immune system and help prevent sickness on the road, which is always better than having to treat the horse after he gets sick.

A potentially serious problem to watch for is that your horse might refuse to drink water while traveling. One solution for short trips of just a night or two is to take containers of water from home that you know your horse will drink. To prevent problems on longer trips, begin adding water in his grain several weeks before you leave. Start with small amounts, and increase it over time until the grain is almost soup-like and he becomes accustomed to eating it this way. Also, put a water bucket by both his hay and grain bins as a dipping bucket. This is what I do for my horses, so I am confident it will help your horse get used to the taste of strange water while you're on the road.

Putting pennies, a little Kool-Aid, a teaspoon of vinegar, or other taste-disguising substances in his water at home and away may help, too. Putting salt in the grain will also encourage your horse to drink away from home.

As the trip date draws near, begin acclimating your horse to the trailer. Take the time to conduct several trailer loading sessions to help prevent those last minute refusal problems. You might even load your horse and have him stand and eat in the trailer while you're working around the house, or even take him on short trips while you run errands around town. Just having him stand tied to the hitching rail at home can put your horse at ease and help prevent nervous pawing in the trailer, too.

Finally, don't wait until the day of your trip to purchase and pack horse supplies, feed, clothes, and other necessary items. It's never a good idea to begin a trip running around to get last minute items. And get some sleep the night before. I know it's hard at times, but if you are tired when you leave, you will be an emotional wreck when you arrive at your destination. This puts extra stress on you and your horse, and can have a negative impact on your safety, health, performance, and enjoyment.

On the road: Once you get on the road, there are a number of things you can do to make the trip safer and more enjoyable. When I'm traveling, I like to leave early and stop early—and I never try to drive more than 500 or 600 miles a day with my horse.

Generally, I don't take my horse out of the trailer during the day unless he seems extra hot, tired, or in need of special care. In warmer months, heat can be a real problem for your horse. Placing an ice block or wet shavings on the floor of the trailer helps keep the horse's legs in good condition. Whenever you can, pull into a gas station and hose your horse down in the trailer to combat heat.

In the event you could not plan your route in advance, pull over once you've found a suitable town and find out if there are fairgrounds, stables, or other horse owners in the area who understand your plight. With a little work, you can find a place for your horse and a motel for you. Remember, a good night's rest is important for both you and your horse.

When nightfall comes, I always try to get my horse out of the trailer and into a clean stall or corral. If you have to leave your horse in the trailer overnight, make sure to open all vents and windows to ensure plenty of fresh air.

If you're traveling in the winter, carry several blankets of different weight to keep your horse warm, as well as a cool-out sheet in case the horse gets too wet. Also, no matter how cold it is, whether moving or stopped, never completely close the trailer up tight with the horse still inside. If the weather gets too cold, just keep adding more blankets to your horse.

If you find moisture on the inside of the trailer's roof or windows, open more windows and check if the horse is hot. If he is not overly warm, open some more windows and consider putting more blankets on the horse. Having moisture present inside the trailer is a serious problem, as it can lead to colds and pneumonia.

Trailering is a normal and necessary part of horse owner-ship—one that takes work and carries plenty of responsibilities. Taking precautions and planning carefully are important aspects to making the process safer for everyone on the road. The tips I've offered, coupled with those from experienced friends and family members, will help you trailer your horse with confidence. That should make your next trip smooth and enjoyable.

John Lyons is one of the founding fathers of the natural horsemanship move-ment, and working together toward equine excellence is his training philosophy. John began training horses in his early twenties and gave his first clinic in 1980 with his long time equine companion, Zip.

To subscribe to *John Lyons' Perfect Horse* magazine, contact Subscription Services, P.O. Box 420234, Palm Coast FL 32142, (800) 829-2521.

LEGEND

Getting There

U Easy access to parking area.

U U Roads will accommodate most truck-trailer combinations.

U U U Some narrow and/or winding roads. Will accommodate most truck-trailer combinations.

U U U U Several miles of narrow and/or winding roads. Will be difficult for certain truck-trailer combinations. Follow recommendations in the trail text.

Parking

U Lots of room to park and turn around; no backing up required.

U U May require backing in or out; few obstacles, which are easy to see and avoid.

U U U Some obstacles; space is adequate, but requires backing up.

U U U U Small and/or limited parking that requires precise backing in or out. May be impossible for larger truck-trailer combinations.

Trail Difficulty

Trail difficulty has been divided into two components—physical ability and training level—to better define the trails listed. For example, a wide, smooth, but very steep trail would require a lot of physical ability, but not much training; a flat trail with many obstacles would require some training, but little physical stamina.

Physical Ability

U Mostly flat, well-groomed, and well-marked trails. Good place to start the out-of-condition and/or inexperienced horse and rider.

U U Obvious trails; may have small hillocks and gullies, and some rocks and/or sandy soil.

U U U Horse and rider should be in good condition to enjoy this ride. Trails generally remote with varied footing and may not be well marked. Some moderate changes in elevation.

U U U U Horse and rider must be in excellent condition to safely navigate and enjoy this ride. Trail blazing may be required. Elevation changes are abrupt and dramatic. Steep climbs and slippery and/or rocky trails should be expected.

Training Level

U Safe for the relatively inexperienced horse and/or rider. Wide trail with few obstacles. No water crossings or bridges.

U U Narrower trail with some obstacles such as fallen branches. Horse and rider should be accustomed to traffic. Horse should be able to back up if necessary to get out of a tight spot.

U U U Horse and rider should be able to negotiate obstacles such as logs, small water crossings, or tree branches. Horse should respond accurately to rider's cues.

U U U U Horse and rider must be well seasoned and able to adapt to the unexpected without losing control. Must be able to blaze new trails, cross water, and handle slippery and unstable footing.

Off-Highway Vehicles and Mountain Bikes

🏁 Expect a few off-highway vehicles (OHVs) and/or mountain bikes.

🏁 🏁 🏁 Trail frequented by off-highway vehicles and/or mountain bikes. Mountain bicyclists tend to ride in the mornings. In areas where cyclists frequent, plan your ride for later in the day to reduce the chance of encounters.

Note: The Off-Highway Vehicle/Mountain Bike listing appears only if applicable to the trail.

Maps

Interstates and Major Highways

Paved Road

Dirt Road

Trail

☞   ☜   ☝   ☟ Points between which distance is indicated

▲ Equestrian camping area   🚗 Parking/staging area

〽 or 〽 Indicates a section of trail that is not shown

·—· Gate

Note: Maps show several trails for each area. Your riding time will vary depending on the route and distance taken, but each area offers a minimum of 2 hours of riding.

Blackrock (Trailhead Camp)
Jordan Hot Springs

Contributed by Jennifer and Rick Fuller

N

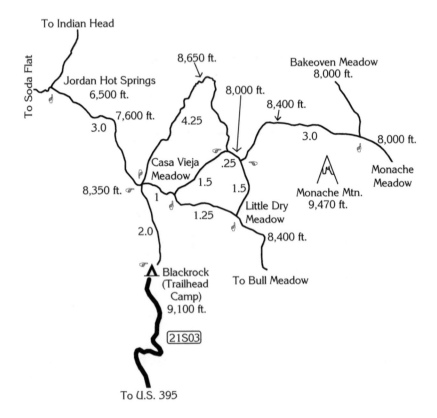

To Indian Head

To Soda Flat

Jordan Hot Springs
6,500 ft.

8,650 ft.

Bakeoven Meadow
8,000 ft.

8,000 ft.

8,400 ft.

7,600 ft.

3.0

4.25

3.0

8,000 ft.

Casa Vieja
Meadow

.25

1.5

1.5

Monache Mtn.
9,470 ft.

Monache
Meadow

8,350 ft.

1

1.25

Little Dry
Meadow

2.0

8,400 ft.

Blackrock
(Trailhead
Camp)
9,100 ft.

To Bull Meadow

21S03

To U.S. 395

Blackrock (Trailhead Camp)
Jordan Hot Springs

Contributed by Jennifer and Rick Fuller

Blackrock trailhead camp is on the north border of the Sequoia National Forest, approximately 40 miles north of Lake Isabella and west of U.S. 395. For information and a fire permit, contact the Blackrock Information Station (619) 376-1666, Wednesday through Monday, 8 A.M. to 4:30 P.M. For maps and additional information, contact the Sequoia National Forest, Cannell Meadow Ranger District, P.O. Box 6, Kernville CA 93238, (619) 376-3781. (The 619 area code will change to 760 on March 22, 1997.)

Jordan Hot Springs is located in the Golden Trout Wilderness in the Inyo National Forest. For maps and additional information, contact the Inyo National Forest, Mount Whitney Ranger District, P.O. Box 8, Lone Pine CA 93545, (619) 876-6200. (The 619 area code will change to 760 on March 22, 1997.)

Hours	None
Fee	None
Getting There	U U U
Parking	U
Hitching Rails/Corrals	Yes/Yes
Trail Difficulty	
Physical Ability	U U U
Training Level	U U to U U U
Elevation	
Blackrock trailhead camp	9,100 feet
Jordan Hot Springs	6,500 feet
Water	
Camp	People: No Horse: No (Water is available at Blackrock Information Station 8 miles south.)
Trail	People: No Horse: Creek
Toilets	Yes, pit
OHVs	Yes, (at Monache Meadow)

Directions:

Take U.S. 395 north of Mojave (south of Lone Pine) to the Kennedy Meadows turnoff (Chimney Peak Recreation Area) and go west 23.9 miles to Kennedy Meadows. Turn left onto National Forest Road 22S05 and continue 12.8 miles to National Forest Road 21S03. Turn right onto 21S03. Go past the Blackrock Information Station and continue 3.5 miles to a fork in the road. Veer left to stay on 21S03 and continue another 4.7 miles to the campground.

Description:

Nestled among towering pines deep within the Sequoia National Forest, Blackrock trailhead camp is a popular starting point for pack trips into the Golden Trout Wilderness. The camp allows a 1-night stay, free of charge on a first-come, first-served basis, to equestrians who want to explore the area. Since the camp is so popular, it's a good idea to bring portable corrals in case you cannot get one of the camp's three or four roomy log corrals.

Fire permits are required and available at the Blackrock Information Station, which is 8 miles south of the camp. If you plan to pack into the back country, you'll also need a wilderness permit. Both permits are free. Water is not available at the camp, so bring your own or fill your containers at the Blackrock Information Station while obtaining your permit(s).

Several years ago, Jordan Hot Springs was a ride-in resort where the lucky traveler could take a long soak in naturally heated spring water and spend the night in a log cabin. The resort closed in 1990 after the establishment of the Golden Trout Wilderness (no commercial ventures are allowed in wilderness areas). The resort is now a registered historical landmark, and most of the log cabins and other buildings remain. A caretaker is present to help preserve them.

Visitors can still enjoy a warm soak at the nearby creek where 110-degree spring water has mixed with creek water and cooled to an agreeable temperature, so do pack a bathing suit and towel.

The trail to Jordan Hot Springs is easy and well marked, with creek water along the way for your horse. You will lose approximately 2,500 feet in elevation over the 5-mile trip and gain it back on the return.

Several other rides are possible from Blackrock trailhead camp, including a trip to Monache Meadow; however, you may encounter off-highway vehicles that are allowed in the area.

Jordan Hot Springs is a "gotta-do" ride for summer heat escapees. Be sure your truck and trailer are in good condition (particularly the brakes) as the road to Blackrock trailhead camp is a long, steep climb.

Photo by Rick Fuller

Cachuma Lake Equestrian Trail

N

Lake
Cachuma

800 ft.

12-mile loop
from parking area

1,000 ft.

900 ft.

Santa
Ynez
River

800 ft.

Live Oak Camp Rd.

To Hwy. 154

Cachuma Lake Equestrian Trail

Located southeast of the Lake Cachuma Recreation Area. Enter via a locked gate (see details under Directions) on Live Oak Camp Road. For more information, contact the Lake Cachuma Recreation Area, Highway 154, Santa Barbara CA 93105, (805) 688-4658, (805) 686-5053, or (805) 686-5055.

Hours
        October 1 through March 31 .... 8 A.M. to 4:30 P.M.
        April 1 through September 30......................... 6 A.M. to 10 P.M.
Fee $5/vehicle
Getting There .... 𝖀 𝖀
Parking .... 𝖀
Hitching Rails/Corrals .... No/No
Trail Difficulty
        Physical Ability.. 𝖀 𝖀
        Training Level.. 𝖀 𝖀
Elevation .... 800 to 1,100 feet
Water
        Staging Area .... People: No Horse: Yes
        Trail .... People: No Horse: River
Toilets .... Yes, pit

Directions:

From Santa Barbara: Take State Highway 154 north 17.4 miles to the entrance of the Lake Cachuma Recreation Area. Turn right (north) into the Recreation Area, drive up to the entrance kiosk, and tell the ranger on duty that you want to ride the Cachuma Lake Equestrian Trail. When you pay the day-use fee, you will receive a permit, trail map, and combination for the locked gate at Live Oak Camp Road.

From the Santa Ynez/Solvang Area: From U.S. 101, take State Highway 154 south 14.5 miles to the entrance of the Lake Cachuma Recreation Area. Turn left (north) into the Recreation Area.

Both: Leave the Recreation Area, turning left (south) onto Highway 154, and travel 5.3 miles to Live Oak Camp Road. Turn left (north) onto Live Oak Camp Road. Make another, immediate, left and continue .1 miles to the locked gate. Use the combination you received to open the gate. After closing the gate, continue another 1 mile to the staging area. Park in the large field on your right.

Description:

The Lake Cachuma Equestrian Trail explores 12 miles of gently rolling, oak-covered hills and offers splendid views of Lake Cachuma a short distance away.

Begin your ride by following the well-marked trail from the parking area to the Santa Ynez River. Based on the time of year, the river may be impassable due to flooding, so do contact the Lake Cachuma Recreation Area for water level information.

Beyond the river, the trail follows a wide ranch road and begins to climb as it circles a small knoll. After reaching the top, the ranch road will fork. Take the left fork and pass through a gate, closing it securely behind you. At this point, the road narrows and becomes more of a trail. The loop begins a short distance from this point, descending into grassy valleys then climbing again for lake views.

The area is characterized by southern oak woodland, valley grassland, and coastal sage scrub plant communities. Coastal sage scrub plants occupy drier areas than chaparral, and the plants don't grow as close together. Several varieties of sage and buckwheat are common. Valley grassland communities include Catalina mariposa lilies. Look for them growing among the wild oats and needlegrass on the drier hillsides during the months of March, April, and May.

Cut off from the ocean's cooling influence, the Cachuma Valley can reach triple-digit temperatures in the summer and early fall. If you live close-by, an early evening ride and picnic dinner may be just the ticket, and you might even see some deer and other wildlife that prefer to feed at dusk.

Also called the Cachuma Loop, the Cachuma Lake Equestrian Trail is a treasure of a find and well worth the effort of driving to the Lake Cachuma Recreation Area office to get the gate combination. (Please note: The trail may be closed during periods of extreme fire danger. Call ahead to confirm.)

Those interested in camping nearby can make a reservation at Upper Oso Campground (see pages 134–137). The Lake Cachuma Recreation Area has two corrals in its overflow camping area that are available only if the overflow area is not being used for nonequestrian campers. The fee is $16 per night and you cannot ride through the park. Contact the number listed above for more information.

Photo by Barbara C. Zimmerman

Cuyamaca Rancho State Park

Contributed by Barbara C. Zimmerman

A 25,000-acre park located in the Laguna Mountains, 40 miles east of San Diego and south of Julian on State Highway 79. For maps and additional information, contact the Cuyamaca Rancho State Park, 12551 Highway 79, Descanso CA 91916, (619) 765-0755. (The 619 area code will change to 760 on March 22, 1997.) Make reservations for Los Caballos Horse Camp (individual campers) and Los Vaqueros Group Camp through DESTINET State and National Park Reservation System, 9450 Carroll Park Drive, San Diego CA 92121, (800) 365-2267, 8 A.M. to 5 P.M. daily.

Los Caballos Horse Camp:

Hours	
Day Use	8 A.M. to Sunset
Overnight	Check-in 2 P.M. Check-out 12 noon
Fee	
Day Use	$5, pay camp host on arrival.
Overnight	$19/night, Sun.–Th. $20/night, Fri. and Sat.
Getting There	♘ ♘
Parking	♘
Hitching Rails/Corrals	
Day Use	Yes/Yes. First-come, first-served.
Overnight	Yes/Yes
Trail Difficulty	
Physical Ability	♘ to ♘ ♘ ♘ ♘
Training Level	♘ to ♘ ♘ ♘ ♘
Elevation	4,760 to 6,512 feet
Water	
Camp	People: Yes Horse: Yes
Trail	People: No Horse: Yes (on most trails)
Toilets	Yes, flush
Bicyclists	Yes, 🚲 (on some trails)

Directions:

Take Interstate 15 to Escondido and exit at State Highway 78 east. Follow State Highway 78 through Escondido and travel 19.9 miles to Ramona. Turn left to stay on State Highway 78 and continue 22.4 miles to Julian. Turn right onto State Highway 79 south and travel 5.8 miles to the intersection with S1, the Sunrise Highway. Keep right and continue on State Highway 79 another 2.3 miles to the park entrance.

Description:

With miles of trails for riders of all levels of expertise and experience, Cuyamaca Rancho State Park comes close to being an equestrian paradise.

Elevations range from 3,200 to 6,512 feet, and the terrain varies from chaparral to dense forests of pine, oak, and incense cedar trees. A variety of wildlife, including black-tailed deer, coyotes, bobcats, raccoons, skunks, and squirrels, live in the park, and rattlesnakes are plentiful. Frequent mountain lion sightings have prompted park officials to request that you do not ride alone. Please see page 17 of the "Safety First" section for some guidelines when riding in mountain lion country, and do report all sightings to park officials.

Trails are well marked and maintained, but if you plan to ride the more remote or difficult trails, check with a park ranger or Mounted Assistance Unit volunteer regarding trail conditions and closures. Trail maps and notices of trail problems are posted at both campgrounds.

Cuyamaca's two equestrian camps are open from late May through October. Check with the park for the exact opening and closing dates. Reservations are a must and difficult to get so plan ahead. DESTINET, the State and National Park Reservation System, allows you to make reservations up to 7 months in advance.

Los Caballos Horse Camp has sixteen individual campsites and a day-use area. Each site comes with two corrals, a table, barbecue, water, and fire ring. The park allows only one horse per corral. You may bring up to four horses, and additional corrals are available in the day-use area on a first-come, first-served basis. The camp host has fire wood for sale, and a pay phone is available. After a grand but sweaty day on the trail, a hot shower will seem like heaven. Showers can be had for 25 cents for 2 minutes (a water conservation effort!), so bring lots of quarters. Restrooms have electrical outlets.

Large groups should inquire about Los Vaqueros Group Camp, which has forty-five corrals, flush toilets, hot showers, a group fire ring, barbecues, and a covered picnic area. The cost is $175 per night and covers up to eighty people, fifty vehicles, and forty-five horses. Electricity and phones are available only at Los Caballos.

The park provides manure buckets and a dumping site at each camp. You are required to rake out your own corral and take the manure to the dumping site.

At both camps, be prepared for nightly raccoon raids. These critters are very persistent and adept at opening coolers, truck bed covers, etc.

The day-use area operates on a first-come, first-served basis and often fills up by late morning on the weekends.

The following pages review three of the park's many trails: the Minshall (Lake Loop) Trail, the Sugar Pine Trail, and the Conejos Trail.

Minshall (Lake Loop) Trail

N

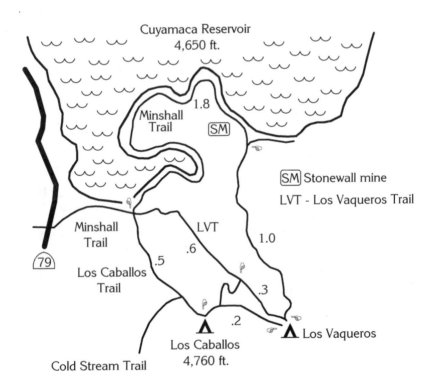

Cuyamaca Reservoir
4,650 ft.

Minshall Trail

1.8

SM

SM Stonewall mine

LVT - Los Vaqueros Trail

Minshall Trail

79

Los Caballos Trail

LVT

.6

.5

1.0

.3

.2

Los Caballos
4,760 ft.

Los Vaqueros

Cold Stream Trail

Minshall (Lake Loop) Trail

Difficulty .... U
Training Level .... U
Distance .... 3.5 miles
Time Estimate .... 1.25 hours
Hikers often encountered

This is a great warm-up trail or an easy stretch for a day after a hard ride. It's also good for the green horse or inexperienced rider. Just prior to sunrise or just after sunset, the trail provides great wildlife watching opportunities.

Follow the Los Caballos Trail out of Los Caballos Horse Camp, or the Los Vaqueros Trail out of Los Vaqueros Group Camp. Both trails end on the Mandy Minshall Trail. Turn right to head toward the lake. The Minshall Trail follows the contours of the lake on the edge of the forest. The footing is mostly soft and sandy with a few rocks. Take care in places where a barbed wire fence comes close to the side of the trail. You'll pass several meadows that are often full of deer. The trail curves away from the lake near Stonewall Mine, which produced more than 2 million dollars worth of gold before it was closed in 1892. A detour allows you to view the historical mine and buildings. Afterward, continue on the Minshall Trail back to the campground.

Sugar Pine Trail

N

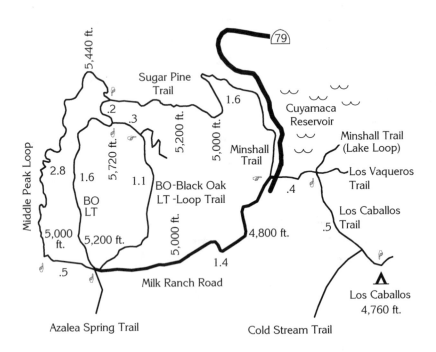

Middle Peak Loop

5,440 ft.

Sugar Pine
Trail

.2

.3

1.6

Cuyamaca
Reservoir

2.8

1.6

5,720 ft.

1.1

5,200 ft.

5,000 ft.

Minshall
Trail

Minshall Trail
(Lake Loop)

Los Vaqueros
Trail

BO-Black Oak
LT -Loop Trail

.4

BO
LT

5,000 ft.

Los Caballos
Trail

.5

5,000
ft.

5,200 ft.

5,000 ft.

4,800 ft.

.5

1.4

.5

Milk Ranch Road

Los Caballos
4,760 ft.

Azalea Spring Trail

Cold Stream Trail

79

Sugar Pine Trail

Difficulty .... 🐾 🐾
Training .... 🐾 🐾
Distance
    Sugar Pine (from camp) .... 2.4 miles
    Middle Peak to Milk Ranch to camp .... 5.5 miles
Time Estimate .... 3 hours

The Sugar Pine Trail is a great ride for a hot day and is rarely used by hikers or bicyclists. Follow the Minshall Trail out to State Highway 79; then cross and pick up the trail on the other side through a break in the fencing on the right side of the pullout for Milk Ranch Road. This narrow trail amidst the tall grass can be difficult to spot, so watch for the break in the fencing.

You'll travel a distance parallel to the highway through the grass and scattered oaks. The trail is narrow—a worn rut below the meadow grade in some areas—and has some loose rock. Just behind the Cuyamaca Lodge Resort buildings, the trail will turn to the left, widen, and start to climb Middle Peak, which is forested in pines, oaks, and aromatic cedars. Actually the remains of an old road, the trail is wide but very rocky and climbs at a steady pace. Near the top of Middle Peak, the footing softens, although a few rocky pockets remain.

At the fork, you can either turn left and pick up the Black Oak Trail to Milk Ranch Road or continue straight ahead on the Sugar Pine Trail to the Middle Peak Fire Road.

The Black Oak Trail is narrow in sections, rocky, and has some steep inclines and declines. Middle Peak Fire Road is wide with gentle grades and great views.

Conejos Trail

N

Minshall Trail

79

Minshall Trail

.4

Los Vaqueros Trail

Los Caballos Trail

.4

4,800 ft.

.1

Black Oak Trail

Middle Peak Fire Road

5,000 ft.

Milk Ranch Road

Los Caballos 4,760 ft.

1.6

.2

Azalea Springs Trail

5,400 ft.
5,600 ft.

Azalea Springs Trail

Cold Stream Trail

3.1

Conejos Trail

5,800 ft.
6,000 ft.

2.0

Cuyamaca Peak Trail

4,600 ft.

6,200 ft.

.5

.8

6,000 ft.

Burnt Pine Fire Trail

To Fern Flat Fire Road

Cold Spring Trail

Cuyamaca Peak 6,512 ft.

3.1

5,800 ft.

5,200 ft.

5,000 ft.

.7

West Mesa Loop Fire Trail

4,280 ft.

1.5

Cold Stream Trail

4,600 ft.

West Mesa Loop Fire Trail

West Mesa Loop Fire Road

Conejos Trail

Difficulty .... ♘♘♘♘
Training Level .... ♘♘♘♘
Distance .... 13 miles
Time Estimate .... 6 hours

For those who want a real challenge and are not afraid of heights, the Conejos Trail is your ticket.

From the horse camps, take the Minshall Trail toward State Highway 79 to Milk Ranch Road. Turn left onto Milk Ranch Road and follow it to the Azalea Springs Fire Road. The Conejos Trail begins about .2 miles up the fire road.

Conejos is a narrow, winding trail that begins in a thick pine and cedar forest and climbs steadily up the north shoulder of Cuyamaca Mountain. As the trees thin, you'll encounter many switchbacks and some trail step-ups, and the footing is difficult with loose rock and boulders to step over, but the views from the north edge of the mountain's shoulder are stunning.

Photo by Barbara C. Zimmerman

From here you'll continue to climb, but the footing will smooth out as you approach Conejos Springs. In the middle of a beautiful fern meadow, Conejos Springs is unlike other park springs because there is no water available for you or your horse.

Continuing on, the forest again thickens as you cross over Cuyamaca's shoulder and travel along the base of the mountain. The trail here is very narrow, with a stretch of riding along the edge of a slope that drops close to 100 feet on your left. The trail improves as you circle around to Cuyamaca's south shoulder.

After crossing a paved Forest Service road, pick up the Burnt Pine Fire Road. Here the trail will widen and begin to descend with some steep parts and a few switchbacks. You'll also encounter some rocky footing.

Burnt Pine Fire Road ends on the West Mesa Loop Fire Road. Turn left and keep descending toward State Highway 79. After crossing the highway, follow the Cold Stream Trail back to camp. You'll find a spring-fed water trough on the Cold Stream Trail that your horses will appreciate after the many hours of climbing fit for a mountain goat!

If you enjoyed the challenge of the Conejos Trail, try the Harvey Moore Trail. It also has loose rock footing and narrow climbs along the edge of a canyon while negotiating trail step-ups. For a 4-hour ride, take the Dyar Springs Trail, or for an 8-hour ride, follow the Harvey Moore Trail all the way back to State Highway 79. The Harvey Moore and Dyar Springs Trails do not directly connect to the Conejos Trail and are not shown on the map on page 48. If you plan to explore them, obtain a park map that shows *all* trails and check trail conditions with the camp host or park rangers as washouts are common.

Scrub Oak
(Queracus dumosa)

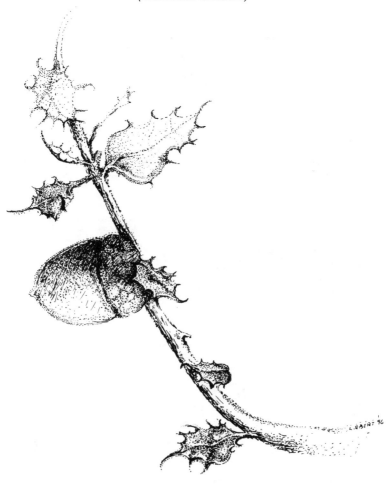

Frank G. Bonelli Regional County Park
(Puddingstone Reservoir)

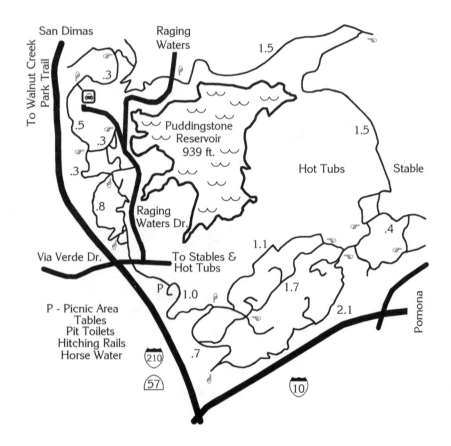

Frank G. Bonelli Regional County Park (Puddingstone Reservoir)

A 1,975-acre park located south of San Dimas and west of the Los Angeles County Fairgrounds. For additional information and maps, contact the Frank G. Bonelli Regional County Park, 120 E. Via Verde Drive, San Dimas CA 91773, (909) 599-8411.

Hours
    March 1 through October 31 .... Sunrise to 10 P.M.
    November 1 through February 28 .... Sunrise to 7 P.M.
Fee .... None. The northwest staging area is outside of park boundaries.
Getting There .... U
Parking .... U
Hitching Rails/Corrals .... Yes/No
Trail Difficulty
    Physical Ability .... U U
    Training Level .... U U
Elevation .... 939 feet at Puddingstone Reservoir
Water
    Staging Area .... People: Yes Horse: Yes
    Trail .... People: No Horse: Yes
Toilets .... Yes, pit
Bicyclists .... Yes, 🚴 (occasional)

Directions:

From Interstate 210, exit at Via Verde Drive and turn left (east). Go .1 miles past the freeway and turn left (north) onto Raging Waters Drive, which is just before the Bonelli Park entrance station. Travel .7 miles on Raging Waters Drive. At the stop sign, veer left and continue another .4 miles. The equestrian staging area is just past the maintenance yard on your left. If it's full, you can park in the Raging Waters overflow parking lot on your right.

Description:

Gently rolling hills; wide, well-maintained trails; and easy access make the Frank G. Bonelli Regional County Park a fine riding destination. Although the staging area is outside of the park proper (you don't have to pay an entrance fee!), it is located next to one of the park's 14 miles of trails. Raging Waters and fishing and boating at Puddingstone Reservoir offer alternative recreation for the nonhorsy family members.

Several looping trails wind through the west and south sections of the park, and a spur near the staging area connects via a tunnel under San Dimas Avenue to the Walnut Creek Park Trail (see page 139). Trails are wide enough to ride two abreast and in the spring are rimmed with hat-high yellow mustard and blankets of blue fern-leaf phacelia (*Phacelia distans*). Other flowers include clumps of purple rock rose, orange bush monkey flower, and yellow broom. Thickets of Arizona ash, oak, and several varieties of pine give pleasant shade. Depending on your route, you'll cross several wooden bridges and eventually reach the tunnel under Via Verde Drive. Framed by bougainvillea, the tunnel does echo some, but it's relatively short and dry and is a good place to expose young horses to the experience.

During the summer, plan to ride early or late as it can get quite hot midday. With the park open until 10 P.M. from March through October, those who live close-by can unwind after a hard day's work with a pleasant evening ride and picnic dinner either at the staging area or along the trail.

The staging area offers a community water trough, pit toilet, garbage cans, drinking fountain, hitching rails, and several picnic tables tucked under a large pepper tree.

For bird-loving equestrians, the following fowl may be spotted:

- Greater roadrunner—one of the 127 species of cuck-oos, it is unique among birds because it can lower its body temperature at night. Its diet consists mostly of reptiles and insects.
- California quail—the state bird, best known for its black head plume. Migrating flocks of common quail are noted in the Book of Exodus as having provided food for the fleeing Israelites.
- Great egret—this magnificent white heron is often seen in shallow water. You can tell this bird is a heron by its long, dark legs and long, yellow bill. Look for the distinctive way it kinks its neck when resting.

Though somewhat noisy due to its proximity to Interstate 210 and Interstate 10, Frank G. Bonelli Regional County Park offers a nice change of pace for area equestrians and makes a pleasant weekend outing for out-of-area visitors.

Hahamongna Watershed Park

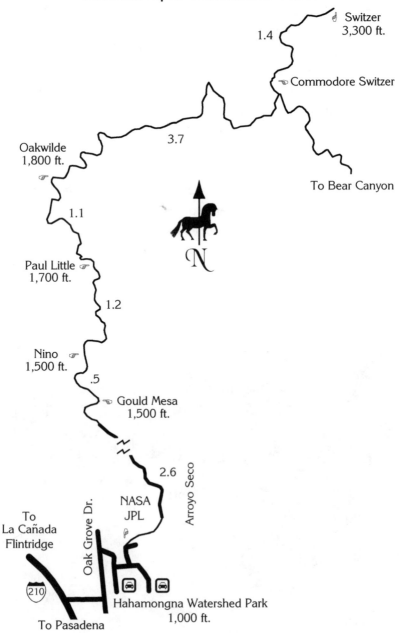

Switzer
3,300 ft.

1.4

Commodore Switzer

3.7

Oakwilde
1,800 ft.

To Bear Canyon

1.1

Paul Little
1,700 ft.

1.2

Nino
1,500 ft.

.5

Gould Mesa
1,500 ft.

2.6

Arroyo Seco

NASA
JPL

Oak Grove Dr.

To
La Cañada
Flintridge

210

Hahamongna Watershed Park
1,000 ft.

To Pasadena

Hahamongna Watershed Park
(Formerly Oak Grove Park)
Arroyo Seco/Gabrielino Trail

Hahamongna Watershed Park is located north of La Cañada Flintridge near Jet Propulsion Lab. For additional information and maps, contact the Hahamongna Operating Company, 1055 W. La Cañada Verdugo Road, Pasadena CA 91103, (818) 585-2000, Monday through Friday, 9 A.M. to 6 P.M.

The Gabrielino Trail traverses the Arroyo Seco and is part of the Angeles National Forest north of Hahamongna Watershed Park. For additional information and maps, contact the U.S. Forest Service, Arroyo Seco Ranger District, Oak Grove Park, Flintridge CA 91011, (818) 790-1151, Monday through Friday, 8 A.M. to 4:30 P.M.

Hours	Sunrise to Sunset
Fee	None
Getting There	U
Parking	U
Hitching Rails/Corrals	No/No
Trail Difficulty	
Physical Ability	U U
Training Level	U to U U
Elevation	
Hahamongna Watershed Park	1,000 feet
Oakwilde Campground	1,800 feet
Switzer	3,300 feet
Water	
Staging Area	People: Yes Horse: Yes
Trail	People: Yes Horse: Creek
Toilets	Yes, flush
Bicyclists	Yes, 🚴

Directions:

Take Interstate 210, the Foothill Freeway, to La Cañada Flintridge. Exit Berkshire Avenue/Oak Grove Drive and go north for .2 miles. At the "T" intersection, turn left onto Oak Grove Drive. Continue .3 miles and make a hairpin right turn into Hahamongna Watershed Park. Smaller rigs can stage at the upper level parking area by continuing straight ahead with the chain-link fence and Oak Grove Drive on your right. There's a loop at the end of the roadway where you can turn around before parking. To stage at the lower parking level, make a left turn after entering the park and go downhill to the parking lot on your right.

Description:

Hahamongna is an ancient Indian word meaning flowing waters and fruitful valley, and it aptly describes a trek up the Arroyo Seco. In the early 1900s, long before the Angeles Crest Highway, this beautiful canyon was one of the most popular vacation spots in the mountains, and remnants of the old road and bridges remain.

A ride up the Arroyo Seco is not only a ride into history but also a relaxing excursion into one of the more luxuriant spots in the San Gabriel Mountains. The path, wide and flat, follows a gently flowing stream as it wends through great stands of alder and sycamore. You'll likely spot several fishermen dipping their poles and perhaps a few children wading in the shallows. Stately oaks, cottonwoods, laurel, and acacia also grow in the moist soil, and poison oak grows unhindered. The stream crosses the trail many times as you make the gentle climb toward Oakwilde Campground—a golden opportunity to teach your dry-land horse how to cross water!

This is an ideal ride for families with younger children because the trail is gentle with few obstacles (except for the water crossings) and wide enough to ride two and three abreast. Do keep an eye out for bicyclists as this is a popular spot.

Begin the ride from the lower Hahamongna parking lot by taking the paved road north toward the ranger station. The dirt trail begins past the ranger station, skirts the E.T.I. Rose Bowl Riders equestrian center, and then follows the east side of the rocky outflow from Arroyo Seco for about 1 mile. There you'll pass a plaque commemorating the 1976 Gabrielino Trail Bicentennial and a fountain where you can fill your canteen before heading into the lush woodland.

Happy Camp Canyon Regional Park

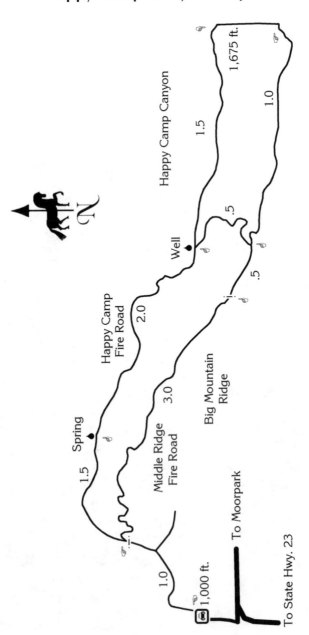

Happy Camp Canyon Regional Park

A 3,000-acre park located in Moorpark and maintained by the Santa Monica Mountains Conservancy for the Eastern Ventura County Conservation Authority. For maps and additional information, contact the Santa Monica Mountains Conservancy, 5750 Ramirez Canyon Road, Malibu CA 90265, (310) 456-5046 x126, Monday through Friday, 9 A.M. to 6 P.M.

Hours	Sunrise to Sunset
Fee	None
Getting There	U
Parking	U
Hitching Rails/Corrals	No/No
Trail Difficulty	
Physical Ability	U to U U
Training Level	U to U U
Elevation	
Staging Area	1,000 feet
Highest Point	1,675 feet
Water	
Staging Area	People: No Horse: No
Trail	People: No Horse: Seasonal
Toilets	Yes, pit
Bicyclists	Yes,

Directions:

Take State Highway 23 to Moorpark and exit at New L.A. Avenue/23 West. Go west for 1.1 miles to Moorpark Avenue; turn right (north). Travel 2.6 miles. Where the road doglegs to the left, continue straight ahead onto Happy Camp Road. Go .1 miles and turn right onto Broadway. Continue .3 miles into the park.

Description:

Riding at Happy Camp—a verdant glen nestled in the mountains between Moorpark and Fillmore—will surely put a smile on your face.

The park consists of Happy Camp Canyon and Big Mountain Ridge that forms the southeast side of the canyon. Two connector trails join the ridge and canyon trails, making two loop rides possible. Happy Camp Fire Road traverses the canyon, passing through several stands of oak trees that offer pleasant shade on a hot day. In the spring, patches of emerald green grass line portions of the trail, enticing you to abandon your boots and stretch out for a nap.

Big Mountain Ridge is chaparral country, and though less shady than Happy Camp Canyon, views of the surrounding area and Simi Valley make it worth a visit.

From the parking area, ride approximately 1 mile along a tree-less path to the canyon gate where the trail splits. The right-hand trail—Middle Ridge Fire Road—climbs Big Mountain Ridge. The left-hand trail—Happy Camp Fire Road—explores the wooded groves of the canyon, including a spring that provides water for many species of plants and animals. Sensitive wildlife areas near the spring are protected by fencing. Please stay on the trail.

Trails are wide and easy to follow, which makes the park a popular destination for both equestrians and bicyclists. When parking your rig, remember to leave enough room for others to get in and out.

Happy Camp Canyon Regional Park can't be beat for that first spring ride, but it's also a fine year-round destination for folks who want a relaxing 3 or 4 hours in the saddle.

HiddEN VallEy PaRk

𝒩

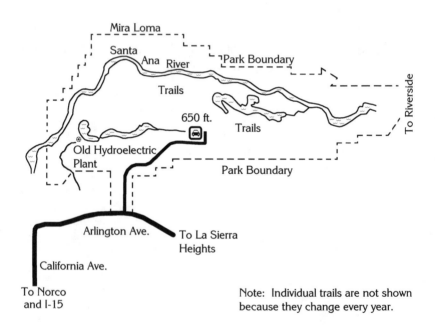

Mira Loma

Santa

Ana River

Park Boundary

Trails

650 ft.

Trails

To Riverside

Old Hydroelectric
Plant

Park Boundary

Arlington Ave.

To La Sierra
Heights

California Ave.

To Norco
and I-15

Note: Individual trails are not shown
because they change every year.

Hidden Valley Park

Part of the Santa Ana River Regional Park, this wildlife preserve is located 4 miles east of Norco in Riverside County. For additional information, contact John Burns, Regional Director, Riverside Regional Parks, 4600 Crestmore, Rubidoux CA 92509, (909) 275-4322, or park aid John Vint at (909) 785-6362.

Hours	8 A.M. to Sunset
Fee	$2/vehicle, exact change required for the fee box.
Getting There	U
Parking	U
Hitching Rails/Corrals	Yes/No
Trail Difficulty	
Physical Ability	U U
Training Level	U to U U U
Elevation	650 feet
Water	
Staging Area	People: No Horse: No
Trail	People: No Horse: Seasonal
Toilets	Yes, pit

Directions:

Take Interstate 15 to Norco; exit at 6th Street and turn east. Travel 1.6 miles to California Avenue and turn left (north). After 1 mile, California Avenue doglegs to the right and becomes North Drive. After .3 miles, North Drive becomes Arlington Avenue. Continue .5 miles on Arlington Avenue and turn left into the park entrance. Travel 1 mile on a wide dirt road to the parking area.

Description:

Think Hawaii. A gentle breeze—alternating between warm and cool—undulates through long tunnels of bamboo. Powder-soft sand muffles the sound of your horse's hoofbeats. Occasional ribbons of water disappear into the tangle of leaves and canes, meandering toward the river that remains hidden, like the exit to an English garden maze.

Located within 3 miles of downtown Norco, Hidden Valley Park is a place of refuge from the hustle and bustle of the city.

From the staging area, you can ride west along two small ponds to the remains of an old hydroelectric plant, which was dismantled when it couldn't keep up with population growth in the area. Or head north and explore the network of bamboo-lined trails along the banks of the Santa Ana River.

The maze of tunnels can be disorienting to some. If you are concerned about getting lost, bring several 12-inch-long strips of plastic gardening tape (used to tie vines to a trellis) to mark your way. Tie them up high so someone won't accidentally pull them down, and be sure to remove them on your way out.

On a blistering day, the Santa Ana River is an inviting place to cool off. However, do take care because it is notorious for quicksand. Cross where the water is moving quickly and only where others have gone before.

When riding in the winter and early spring, check with the park office for river conditions. As the river swells with rain and melting snow, it becomes treacherous. Every year, this same runoff rearranges the maze of bamboo tunnels—creating a new labyrinth of trails that awaits your exploration.

Hole-in-the-Wall
Black Canyon Group Campground

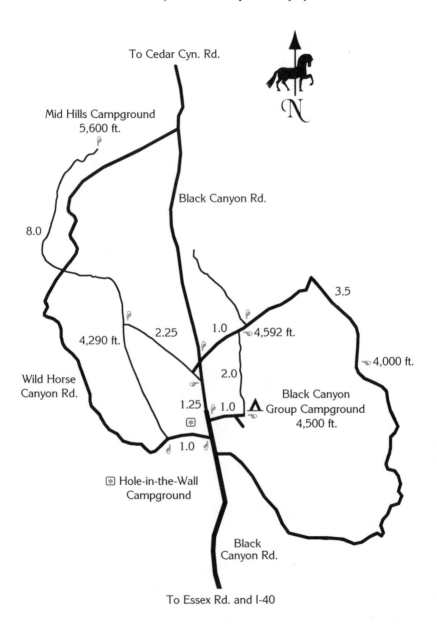

To Cedar Cyn. Rd.

N

Mid Hills Campground
5,600 ft.

Black Canyon Rd.

8.0

3.5

4,290 ft.

2.25   1.0   4,592 ft.

4,000 ft.

Wild Horse
Canyon Rd.

2.0

1.25   1.0   Black Canyon
Group Campground
4,500 ft.

1.0

Hole-in-the-Wall
Campground

Black
Canyon Rd.

To Essex Rd. and I-40

Hole-in-the-Wall
Black Canyon Group Campground

Located 100 miles east of Barstow off Interstate 40 in the Mojave National Preserve. Equestrian camping is by reservation only. For maps, additional information, and reservations, contact the National Park Service, 22 East Main Street
#202, Barstow CA 92311, (619) 255-8801, Monday through Friday, 8 A.M. to 5
P.M. (The 619 area code will change to 760 on March 22, 1997.)

Hours
    Day Use .... Sunrise to Sunset
    Overnight .... Check-out 12 noon
Fee
    Day Use .... None
    Overnight .... $20/night for one of the
                                         two group campsites.
Getting There .... 🐎
Parking .... 🐎
Hitching Rails/Corrals .... Yes/Yes
Trail Difficulty
    Physical Ability... 🐎 🐎 to 🐎 🐎 🐎 🐎
    Training Level.. 🐎 to 🐎 🐎 🐎
Elevation at Black Canyon Campground .... 4,500 feet
Water
    Camp .... People: Horse:
                                          (NPS is working on water
                                          lines. Call to determine
                                          status.)
    Trail .... People: No Horse: No
Toilets .... Yes, pit

Directions:

    Take Interstate 15 north to Barstow where Interstate 40 begins.
Take Interstate 40 east 98.7 miles to Essex Road; exit and go
north. Travel 10.2 miles and then turn right onto Black Canyon
Road. Continue 9.8 miles to the Hole-in-the-Wall Fire Center sign.
Turn right onto the dirt road and go .8 miles to the fire center

(station). Veer left at the "Y" and continue .2 miles to the Black Canyon Group Campground. Equestrians are not allowed in the Hole-in-the-Wall family campground on the west side of Black Canyon Road.

Description:

Wide open spaces and a chance to experience the desert's subtle, silent palette await the visitor to Hole-in-the-Wall. Surrounded by rugged walls of rhyolite, a form of crystallized red lava ash, it's easy to imagine the area as an outlaw's hideout. Indeed, Hole-in-the-Wall was named by one of Butch Cassidy's gang for its resemblance to his old Wyoming haunt.

The first thing you'll notice is the absence of noise. On a recent visit, not even the rumble of a car on Black Canyon Road a mile away could pierce the unconditional quiet. At night, as you ponder billions of stars flickering in the black bowl overhead, the stillness becomes cosmic.

From the Black Canyon Group Campground, you can ride in almost any direction. To explore Wild Horse Canyon, ride north up the wash approximately 2 miles until you reach a wide dirt road. Turn left onto the dirt road and continue another mile until you intersect the dirt portion of Black Canyon Road. Cross Black Canyon Road and continue west on the dirt road. It veers north for approximately 2 miles and eventually connects with the Wild Horse Canyon Trail to Mid Hills Campground. You can also ride along Wild Horse Canyon Road—a 12-mile road that gives spectacular glimpses of Kelso Dunes, Devil's Playground, the Providence Mountains, and the volcanic mesas and spires of Wild Horse Mesa. Near Hole-in-the-Wall Campground, the road passes through a striking cactus garden.

Be sure to carry a pair of pliers or hemostats to remove cactus spines from your horse's legs. We encountered some very nasty chollo while riding cross-country.

Black Canyon Group Campground has six stout pipe corrals, each with a hitching rail in front of it. In between every two corrals is a water spigot—the old-fashioned kind with a large pump handle that you lift to turn on the water. You can't attach a hose, so be prepared to carry buckets.

There are no fire rings or stoves, and collecting or cutting wood is not allowed. You may build a contained fire—in a metal container such as a barbecue—using charcoal or wood brought from home. Be sure to properly dispose of the ashes. You'll have to collect and remove your horse's manure as the campground has only one small garbage can that is not designed to hold manure. The two pit toilets are adequate if the camp is not full; otherwise, be prepared for lines. The only tables are located some distance from the corrals, clustered together under a wood patio.

The campground is fully fenced to keep out range cattle. Be sure to close all gates behind you, and be prepared to encounter cattle on the trail.

Joshua Tree National Park
Black Rock Canyon

N

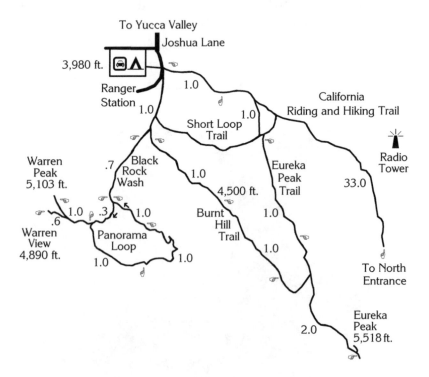

To Yucca Valley

Joshua Lane

3,980 ft.

Ranger Station

1.0

1.0

Short Loop Trail

California Riding and Hiking Trail

Radio Tower

Warren Peak 5,103 ft.

.7   Black Rock Wash

1.0

4,500 ft.

Eureka Peak Trail

33.0

1.0   .3   1.0

.6

Warren View 4,890 ft.

Panorama Loop

Burnt Hill Trail

1.0

1.0

1.0   1.0

To North Entrance

2.0

Eureka Peak 5,518 ft.

Joshua Tree National Park
Black Rock Canyon

Joshua Tree National Park consists of 793,000 acres and is located east of Palm Springs. Entrance to Black Rock Canyon is via Joshua Lane in the town of Yucca Valley. For maps and additional information, contact the National Park Service, Joshua Tree National Park, 74485 National Park Drive, Twentynine Palms CA 92277-3597, (619) 367-7511, 8 A.M. to 5 P.M. daily. Or call (619) 365-9585 for the Black Rock Canyon Ranger Station. (The 619 area code will change to 760 on March 22, 1997.)

Hours
    Day Use .... Sunrise to Sunset
    Overnight .... None
Fee
    Day Use .... None
    Overnight .... $10/night. No corrals.
Getting There .... 🐴🐴
Parking .... 🐴
Hitching Rails/Corrals .... Yes/No
Trail Difficulty
    Physical Ability .... 🐴🐴 to 🐴🐴🐴🐴
    Training Level .... 🐴 to 🐴🐴🐴
Elevation at Black Rock Campground .... 3,980 feet
Water
    Camp .... People: Yes Horse: Yes
    Trail .... People: No Horse: No
Toilets .... Yes, flush

Directions:

From Interstate 10, exit at State Highway 62, the Twentynine Palms Highway, and go north. Continue 22 miles to State Highway 247 in the town of Yucca Valley and turn right (south) onto Joshua Lane. (State Highway 247 becomes Joshua Lane south of Twentynine Palms Highway.) Travel 4.5 miles, through a residential area, then turn right at the "T" intersection onto San Marino

Drive. Continue .4 miles to the park entrance and turn right. Make an immediate left into the equestrian parking/camping area.

Description:

Situated at nearly 4,000 feet, Black Rock Canyon is a potential late spring/early summer desert riding and camping destination. The equestrian camping area is nothing more than a parking lot the size of a football field that is partially surrounded by a low, split-rail fence. With several openings in the fence for trails and driveways, a horseman would never think of the parking lot as a corral—in spite of park personnel who describe it as such. If you want to camp, bring portable corrals or tie your horses to the trailer.

Three long hitching rails are provided as well as three old-fashioned water faucets with long handles that are lifted to turn on the water. You can't attach a hose to the faucet, so be prepared to carry buckets for your horses.

You are responsible for disposing manure in the dumpster that is provided.

A few picnic tables are clustered under some Joshua trees in the northeast corner of the otherwise shadeless parking area. Folks who tent camp will have a long walk to the toilets. Campfires are allowed only in provided fire pits. Bring your own wood. You can cook with a camp stove or portable grill.

Given these limitations, Black Rock Canyon is a great place to experience the high desert. The best time to visit is spring, when winter cooling lingers and drought-tolerant flowers burst into bloom. In the fall and winter, the low sun casts a golden light on the landscape. Winter can bring snow—flurries that coat familiar plants with an alien-looking white fuzz. It doesn't seem possible in this land where summer temperatures regularly reach 120 degrees Fahrenheit and the plants are spiny and tough.

Joshua Tree National Park is composed of a fragile web of plants and animals with the Joshua tree (*Yucca brevifolia*) at the center. Birds nest in the tree and feed on termites and other insects infesting it. Fallen limbs provide a home for yucca night lizards, who in turn eat the termites. Stink bugs nibble on the decaying Joshua fibers helping the termites—and inadvertently the night lizards—who are then eaten by owls and snakes. Then along comes a coyote—the desert's most successful opportunist. *

Black Rock Canyon offers several miles of trails through great stands of Joshua trees. Begin your ride from the east end of the equestrian campground, and then turn south into Black Rock Wash. At each trail intersection you'll find a wood post etched with the trail initials, making it easy to explore without getting lost.

---

* For more information about California deserts, see Michael Parfit, "California Desert Lands: A Tribute to Sublime Desolation," *National Geographic*, May 1996, 54–79.

The trail in Black Rock Wash is composed of soft sand that is bronzed at sunset and tinged rose at sunrise. Joshua trees give way to oaks and other more water-needy plants as you gradually ascend the canyon.

For great views of the Black Rock Canyon area and the desert to the north, try the Panorama Loop. The last half mile or so near the eastern curve of the loop is quite steep and narrow with soft footing; otherwise, it's a beautiful ride with a 50-mile panorama at the highest point. Warren View and Warren Peak face west toward the snow-capped San Bernardino Mountains, Desert Hot Springs, and Morongo Valley.

When you ride in the desert, always carry plenty of water—and drink it. Wear sunscreen, a hat, and sunglasses. Insect repellent for both horse and rider is a good idea, too. Give a wide berth to snakes and scorpions—they will usually get out of your way if you let them. And watch out for the many-branched jumping chollo. From a distance, the copious spines glow a brilliant yellowish-white. Close up, branches are easily detached, hence the name jumping chollo. Carry a pair of pliers (needle nose are best), narrow-tined comb, or hemostat to remove any spines from your horse's legs. For stubborn spines, soak the skin with vinegar first.

White Nightshade
(Solanum)

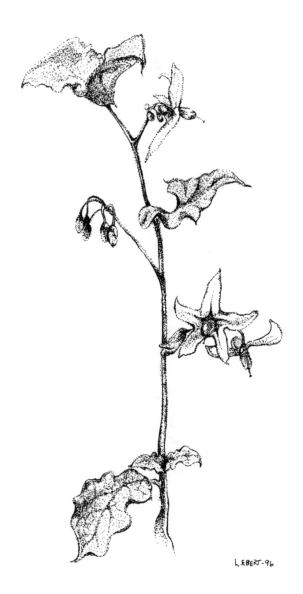

L.EBERT-96

Joshua Tree National Park
Ryan Campground
The California Riding and Hiking Trail

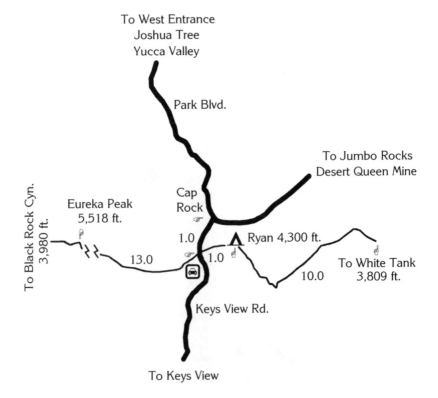

Joshua Tree National Park
Ryan Campground
The California Riding and Hiking Trail

Joshua Tree National Park consists of 793,000 acres located east of Palm Springs. The entrance to Ryan Campground is via the West Entrance Station. For maps and additional information, contact the National Park Service, Joshua Tree National Park, 74485 National Park Drive, Twentynine Palms CA 92277-3597, (619) 367-7511, 8 A.M. to 5 P.M. daily. (The 619 area code will change to 760 on March 22, 1997.)

Hours
    Day Use .... Sunrise to Sunset
    Overnight .... None
Fee
    Park Entrance Fee .... $5 (good for 7 days)
    Overnight .... No extra charge. No corrals.
Getting There .... 𝕌 𝕌
Parking .... 𝕌 𝕌 to 𝕌 𝕌 𝕌
Hitching Rails/Corrals .... Yes/No
Trail Difficulty
    Physical Ability .... 𝕌 𝕌 to 𝕌 𝕌 𝕌 𝕌
    Training Level .... 𝕌 to 𝕌 𝕌
Elevation at Ryan Campground .... 4,300 feet
Water
    Camp .... People: No   Horse: No
    Trail .... People: No   Horse: No
Toilets .... Yes, pit

Directions:

From Interstate 10, exit at State Highway 62, the Twentynine Palms Highway, and go north. Continue 27.8 miles to Park Boulevard and turn right (south). Continue 5.1 miles to the entrance station. From the kiosk, continue on Park Boulevard for 10.5 miles to the intersection with Keys View Road.

For Day-Use Parking: Turn right onto Keys View Road and continue 1.1 miles to a large turnout on your right, located on the California Riding and Hiking Trail.

To Ryan Campground (for overnight): At the Keys View Road intersection, continue straight ahead on Park Boulevard for .5 miles to the Ryan Campground entrance. Turn right and travel .8 miles on a dirt road into the campground proper.

Description:

This section of the park, nestled between the Pinto and Little San Bernardino Mountains, is drier and more desert-like than Black Rock Canyon. Spectacular granite monoliths and boulder clusters dominate much of the landscape. Cap Rock and Ryan Mountain are composed of monzonite granite—a light gray igneous rock rich in quartz crystals and containing approximately 10 percent dark minerals. Igneous rocks are formed by cooling lava, and granite is one of the most commonly exposed rocks.

You'll still see plenty of Joshua trees, but the companion plants—such as cresote bush, cotton thorn, and Indian rice grass—are more drought tolerant than those at Black Rock. Along the trail west of the day-use parking area, a few junipers and piñon pines manage to eke out a living.

Ryan is a dry camp with areas designated for horses but no corrals. Garbage and recycle bins, tables, fire pits, and pit toilets are provided. Bring plenty of water for you and your horse, and be sure to clean up your horse's manure.

The equestrian "main drag" is the California Riding and Hiking Trail that passes through the park, roughly east to west. From the day-use parking area, the trail west gently climbs the foothills of Quail Mountain. You can ride all the way to Black Rock Canyon some 18 miles away. East of Ryan, the trail follows the flat Queen

Valley, veering north toward Jumbo Rocks and the remains of the Desert Queen Mine—a product of the California Gold Rush.

Whenever you ride in the desert, carry plenty of water and protect yourself from the sun. Rattlesnakes, including the generally nocturnal sidewinder, live in the park. They will usually get out of your way if you let them. Pack a pair of pliers (needle nose are best), narrow-tined comb, or hemostat to remove chollo spines from your horse's legs.

At night, the stillness of the desert encompasses you. The sublime vastness and brilliant heavens above can make you feel small and frail. But that's what the desert is all about—a dazzling show guaranteed to reawaken your excitement and appreciation of the great outdoors.

Malibu Creek State Park
Phantom Trail

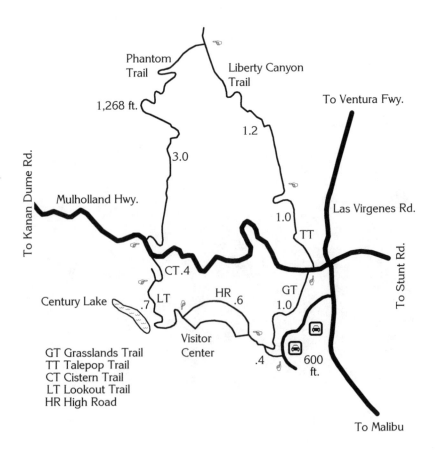

Phantom Trail

Liberty Canyon Trail

To Ventura Fwy.

1,268 ft.

1.2

3.0

To Kanan Dume Rd.

Mulholland Hwy.

Las Virgenes Rd.

1.0

TT

CT .4

GT

HR .6

1.0

To Stunt Rd.

Century Lake

.7   LT

600 ft.

Visitor Center

.4

To Malibu

GT Grasslands Trail
TT Talepop Trail
CT Cistern Trail
LT Lookout Trail
HR High Road

Malibu Creek State Park
Phantom Trail

Malibu Creek State Park consists of 10,000 acres in the Santa Monica Mountains, south of Agoura Hills. For additional information and detailed maps, contact the Department of Parks and Recreation, Angeles District, Malibu Sector, 1925 Las Virgenes Road, Calabasas CA 91302, (818) 880-0350, Monday through Friday, 8 A.M. to 5 P.M. The Mountain Parks Information Hotline is (800) 533-7275.

Hours	8 A.M. to Sunset
Fee	$5/vehicle. Have exact change during the week.
Getting There	
Parking	
Hitching Rails/Corrals	No/No
Trail Difficulty	
Physical Ability	U to U U U U
Training Level	U U
Elevation	
Parking Area	600 feet
Phantom Peak	1,268 feet
Water	
Staging Area	People: Yes Horse: Yes
Trail	People: No Horse: Creek
Toilets	Yes, flush

Directions:

Take U.S. 101, the Ventura Freeway, to Agoura Hills. Exit at Las Virgenes Road and go south. Travel 3.3 miles and then turn right (west) into the park.

Description:

Master trail builder Ron Webster gave the Phantom Trail its name after being told it followed an old stagecoach route. Given the terrain, he wondered if either the truth was lost in history or was a phantom of someone's imagination—and thus the name was born.

The Phantom Trail is one of several trails in the park and connects with other trails to form an 8-mile loop. Sections of the trail pass through thick brush that is loaded with ticks. Be sure to apply a tick repellent to both you and your horse, and check for ticks after the ride. You'll also encounter some poison oak crowding the trail. Wear a long-sleeve shirt to help prevent a nasty outcome.

Begin your ride from the main parking lot and head west on Crags Road for a short distance. After crossing Las Virgenes Creek, turn right onto the Grasslands Trail that roughly parallels Malibu Canyon Road through undulating wild oats and grand valley oak trees. One of the largest of the American oaks and a California native, the valley oak once covered large areas of fertile flatlands. Now only a few isolated stands remain.

You might see a feathery, fern-like plant tucked among the wild oats. That's fennel, a non-native plant that park staff is trying to eradicate. The Grasslands Trail ends at Mulholland Highway. Cross the highway, taking care to watch and listen for speeding cars and motorcycles, and pick up the Talepop Trail on the other side.

The Talepop Trail skirts a section of private property and eventually connects with Liberty Canyon Road, a wide dirt road. Continue along Liberty Canyon Road for approximately 1.2 miles; then make a left onto the Phantom Trail. A permanent trail sign is in the works. Meanwhile, watch for a well-cleared dirt path marked by a blue, plastic tape flag.

The trail dips down to a year-round creek and then begins to climb "phantom peak." Notice the abrupt change in vegetation as you leave the flat valley floor. Here's where you'll encounter ticks and poison oak twined in the thick chaparral. Walnut trees and scrub oaks cling to the rocky hillsides. Ceanothus, sage, and bush monkey flowers are common. Other wildflowers to look for include farewell-to-spring, paintbrush, and bush sunflower (quarter-sized flowers with a black center).

The Phantom Trail climbs steadily for approximately 2 miles to the peak's 1,268-foot crest. Here you'll have a near 360-degree view of the park and beyond. The trail follows the ridge line for a short distance, then drops rapidly, and ends at Mulholland Highway. Cross the road and travel east along the shoulder a few yards; then turn right onto the Cistern Trail. Just south of the highway is the rectangular, concrete cistern for which the trail was named. A stand of 8-foot-tall Matilija poppies grows nearby. According to Milt McAuley, author of *Wildflowers of the Santa Monica Mountains*, these plants were introduced many years ago, probably from rootstock taken from the Cuyama area in Santa Barbara County.

The Cistern Trail connects with the Lookout Trail that passes Century Lake, which was formed in 1901 when the Crags Country Club members built a dam on Malibu Creek.   Over the years, a freshwater marsh has developed and is home to many migratory birds.

The Lookout Trail ends at Crags Road near the Visitor's Center.   The wood-framed structure was built in 1926 and originally was one of the Crags Country Club homes. It now houses a small bookstore and museum, which are worth a visit (you can tie your horse to a tree near the entrance). From the museum, take either the High Road or Crags Road back to the parking lot.

Malibu Creek State Park offers over 30 miles of trails through an area rich in history. Although bicyclists are not allowed on the Phantom Trail or the connecting trails listed here, they occasionally stray where they are prohibited. Back-country areas are evacuated and closed to the public during periods of high fire danger. If you plan to ride in the late summer and fall, call (310) 454-2372 for fire closure information.

Coffee Fern
(Pellaea andromedifolia)

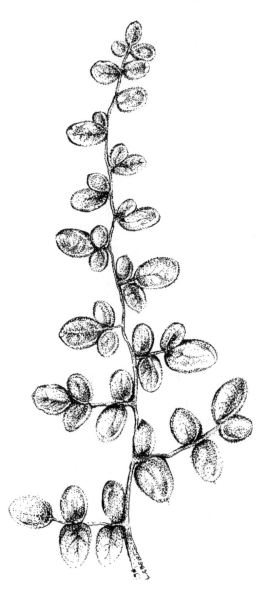

Manzanita Horse Camp

N

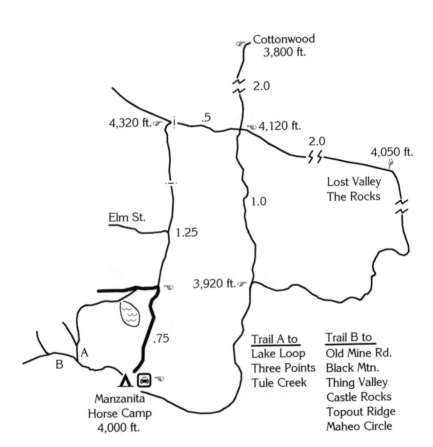

Cottonwood
3,800 ft.

2.0

4,320 ft.   .5   4,120 ft.

2.0

4,050 ft.

Lost Valley
The Rocks

1.0

Elm St.

1.25

3,920 ft.

.75

Trail A to	Trail B to
Lake Loop	Old Mine Rd.
Three Points	Black Mtn.
Tule Creek	Thing Valley
	Castle Rocks
	Topout Ridge
	Maheo Circle

A
B

Manzanita
Horse Camp
4,000 ft.

Manzanita Horse Camp

A private facility located near Live Oak Springs, approximately 50 miles east of San Diego off Interstate 8. For additional information and reservations, contact Manzanita Horse Camp, P.O. Box 1302, Boulevard CA 91905, (619) 766-4070.

Hours
    Day Use .... Sunrise to Sunset
    Overnight .... None
Fee
    Day Use $3/horse
    Overnight .... $10/night no hookups, $20/night full hookups. Includes two 12-by-12-foot pipe corrals. Additional horses $2/night.
Getting There .... 🐎
Parking .... 🐎
Hitching Rails/Corrals .... No/Yes
Trail Difficulty
    Physical Ability .... 🐎 🐎 to 🐎 🐎 🐎 🐎
    Training Level .... 🐎 to 🐎 🐎 🐎
Elevation at Campground .... 4,000 feet
Water
    Camp .... People: Yes Horse: Yes
    Trail .... People: No Horse: Seasonal
Toilets .... Yes, flush

Directions:

Take Interstate 8 to Live Oak Springs. Exit at Live Oak Springs Road and go south onto Olde Highway 80. Continue 1.9 miles on Olde Highway 80 to Royal Road; turn left. Royal Road becomes Live Oaks Trail. Continue 4.6 miles on Live Oaks Trail, across two cattle guards to where the pavement ends and the road forks. Take the right dirt road fork and follow the "Horse Camp & Arena" sign 1 mile into the campground.

Description:

With over eighty corrals, hookups, flush toilets, showers, and many miles of well-marked trails, Manzanita Horse Camp is a fantastic place to spend a long weekend—or longer if you can manage. Other amenities include a kid's play area, group fire pit, and dump station. Garbage cans are located by the toilets. A large area has been set aside for groups and boasts a lighted stage and serving counter.

Corrals are clustered in groups of ten to fifteen around the perimeter of the camp. Each cluster is serviced by a hose bib, and Manzanita provides the hose. Many of the thirty-three, full hookup camping sites are shaded with pine trees and both evergreen and deciduous oaks. Most have tables, stoves, and fire pits. You are asked to rake your horse's manure into the aisle, where it will be collected for disposal.

Manzanita is a working cattle ranch, and you may encounter loose cattle while riding.

Two trailheads lead north from the campground. The west trailhead (west of the main campground) offers several riding options, including a gentle, 2-hour Lake Loop that is a great warm-up ride for the out-of-condition horse and/or rider.

From the Lake Loop, you can see Juancinto's Cemetery tucked beneath a huge oak tree. This is an active cemetery where loved ones are remembered with colorful silk and tissue flowers.

Another place you can explore from the west trailhead is Thing Valley, which is approximately 7 miles northwest at the foot of the Laguna Mountains. The trail crosses several ravines, so expect a good workout even though you gain only 1,000 feet or so in elevation.

The east trailhead begins to the right of the arena by the main house. You'll be greeted by a carved wood sign that reads, "Horse Trails, Please Use"—a welcome sentiment in a time when many places are restricting equestrian access. Follow the soft sand trail to the intersection with the Lake Loop Trail and then continue north (straight ahead) to Elm Street.

Elm Street is a rather proper name for a rarely used dirt track that disappears into dense chaparral. In fact, you'd ride right past if not for a tiny sign pointing it out. Beyond Elm Street, you'll pass through two gates; make a right turn (east) and head toward Lost Valley, home of The Rocks.

The Rocks are clusters of bowling-ball-to-condo-sized monoliths rising skyward in an otherwise homogeneous, dusty-green landscape. In the evening, as the sun drops below the horizon, The Rocks glow like freshwater pearls. Look for one shaped like an eagle's beak.

From Lost Valley, you can continue east, looping back to camp, but do check with the Manzanita staff to make sure the trails are open. Otherwise, return the way you came.

If you're looking for almost guaranteed overnight camping space (even on holiday weekends) and plenty of riding, then Manzanita Horse Camp is your ticket to fun and adventure.

Catalina Mariposa Lily
(Calochortus catalinae)

Mount Gower Open Space Preserve

Contributed by Barbara C. Zimmerman

N

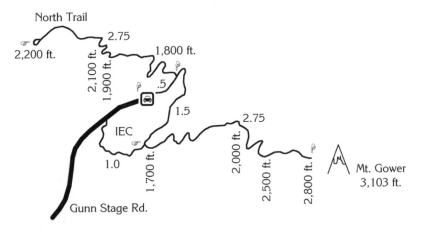

North Trail

2.75

2,200 ft.

1,800 ft.

2,100 ft.

1,900 ft.

.5

1.5

2.75

IEC

1.0

1,700 ft.

2,000 ft.

2,500 ft.

2,800 ft.

Mt. Gower
3,103 ft.

Gunn Stage Rd.

To Ramona

Mount Gower Open Space Preserve

Contributed by Barbara C. Zimmerman

A 1,574-acre preserve located southeast of Ramona, 17090 Gunn Stage Road, Ramona CA 92065. For additional information, contact Dave Martinez, Supervisor, Open Space Division, County of San Diego Department of Parks and Recreation, 1640 Weld Boulevard, El Cajon CA 92020, (619) 579-4436, fax (619) 562-9719.

Hours
    Day Use .... 8:30 A.M. to Sunset
    Overnight .... By reservation and special
                                                                 arrangement. Contact
                                                                 Dave Martinez.
    The park staging area is closed during August. You may stage outside of
    the park and ride in through an access gate.
Fee
    Day Use .... None
    Overnight .... Contact Dave Martinez
Getting There .... U
Parking .... U
Hitching Rails/Corrals .... No/No
Trail Difficulty
    Physical Ability .... U U to U U U
    Training Level .... U to U U U
Elevation
    Staging Area .... 1,700 feet
    Mount Gower Trail's End .... 2,800 feet
Water
    Staging .... People: Yes Horse: Yes
    Trail .... People: No Horse: Seasonal
Toilets .... Yes, pit
Bicyclists .... Yes, 🏁 (uncommon)

Directions:

From San Diego: Take Interstate 15 to Poway (north of Miramar). Take the Poway Road exit and go east. Travel 9 miles until the road ends at State Highway 67. Turn left (north) onto State Highway 67 and continue 9.3 miles into the town of Ramona. Turn right (south) onto 10th Street.

From Escondido and North: Take Interstate 15 to Escondido and exit at State Highway 78 east. Follow State Highway 78 through Escondido and travel 19.9 miles to Ramona where State Highway 78 intersects State Highway 67. After the intersection, State Highway 78 becomes 10th Street. Continue straight ahead on 10th Street.

Both: 10th Street will become San Vicente Road. Follow San Vicente Road for 6 miles to San Diego Country Estates; turn left onto Gunn Stage Road. Travel 1.8 miles to preserve entrance.

Description:

The main trail begins with gently rolling hills for about 1.5 miles and then climbs via switchbacks toward the peak of Mount Gower. As you start the climb, you'll cross an oak-lined creek that runs from December through May—a good place to allow your horse to drink. The creek feeds a waterfall that can be seen from sections of the trail. The trail winds through sage and chaparral, giving way to beautiful rock outcroppings near the top where the view is spectacular—all the way to the ocean on a clear day. The trail is wide (3 to 4 feet) and well maintained. Footing is good with some moderately rocky areas and some sandy stretches, but it can become hard in the late summer. Soils are a mixture of igneous rock components, granodiorite rock components, and ancient sedimentary deposits.

Rattlesnakes, coyotes, bobcats, desert horned lizards (a.k.a. "horneytoads"), and kangaroo rats live in the reserve, and mountain lions have been sighted at higher elevations. Rock outcrops support hawks and other birds of prey.

For a shorter ride, just before crossing the creek, turn right onto a narrower trail and loop around to the San Diego Country Estates International Equestrian Center (known as the IEC by local residents) and up Gunn Stage Road. Before taking this loop, you must stop at the IEC and sign a liability waiver in order to ride on its private property. This loop is particularly good for out-of-condition or inexperienced horses and/or riders as the climbs and descents are milder than those of Mount Gower.

A third trail option is the North Trail, suitable for more advanced horses and riders than either the Mount Gower Trail or the IEC Loop. The North Trail traverses some very steep declines into narrow "V" canyons and back out, and there may be water to cross in the bottoms of these canyons. Continuing, the trail switchbacks to the top of the ridge, then takes you back the same way. Much of this ride is over loose rock and hard ground.

With three trails to choose from, your can tailor your ride to your level of conditioning and experience. This makes the Mount Gower Open Space Preserve a special place worth visiting.

Photo by Barbara C. Zimmerman

Ojai Valley Trail

Ojai Valley Trail

Located north of Ventura along State Highway 33 between Foster Park and Soule Park. For detailed maps and additional information, contact the County of Ventura, General Services Agency, Recreation Services, L #1030, 800 South Victoria Avenue, Ventura CA 93009, (805) 654-3951, Monday through Thursday, 8:30 A.M. to 2 P.M.

For Foster Park and Soule Park:
Hours
    Summer 4/1-10/31 .... 7:30 A.M. to 8:00 P.M.
    Winter 11/1-3/31 .... 7:30 A.M. to 5:30 P.M.
Fee .... $2 per vehicle, weekends and holidays.
Getting There .... U
Parking .... U
Hitching Rails/Corrals .... No/No
Trail Difficulty
    Physical Ability .... U
    Training Level .... U U
Elevation
    Foster Park .... 165 feet
    Soule Park .... 825 feet
Water
    Staging Area .... People: Yes Horse: Yes
    Trail .... People: No Horse: Seasonal
Toilets .... Yes, flush
Bicyclists .... Yes, 🚲 🚲 🚲 (on pedestrian side of trail)

Directions:

To Foster Park: Take U.S. 101, the Ventura Freeway, to Ventura; then go north on State Highway 33. Travel 5.6 miles and exit at Casitas Vista Road. Turn right onto Casitas Vista Road and travel .1 miles. Just before crossing the old concrete and stone bridge, turn right into the park entrance. The equestrian staging area is at the end of the road. (You can also stage at Soule Park, but the park is not as nice.)

Description:

The Ojai Valley Trail is a state-of-the-art, rail-to-trail conversion that should not be missed by anyone interested in alternative trail technology. Rail-to-trail projects, which are quite popular in the East, convert old railroad easements into multiuse trails. The Ojai Valley Trail is one of a handful of these conversions located on the West Coast. Railroad easements make excellent multiuse trails due to their width and gentle grade, and the Ojai Valley Trail makes good use of both.

Divided down the middle by a post and rail fence, the Ojai Valley Trail neatly separates equestrians from pedestrian and bicycle traffic—an important safety feature for multiuse trails. Trail planners paved only the pedestrian side. The equestrian path is dirt with occasional sections of wood chips and shredded bark.

The trail, which is 8.8 miles long, is tucked between the Ventura River on the west and State Highway 33 on the east. Automobile noise is somewhat of a detraction, and you'll cross several paved streets that are well marked and signed for equestrian crossing.

Great white egrets and other water-loving birds live along the Ventura River and can be seen from the trail. Stands of oak, pine, and sycamore provide patches of shade as you ride, and spring flowers include yellow broom, yellow and white acacia, and blue lupine. Winter rains may force closure of the trail, so do call ahead for trail conditions.

Shaded by giant sycamore and eucalyptus trees, Foster Park makes a pleasant after-ride picnic spot. Picnic tables, stoves, and garbage cans are provided. For large groups, a Santa Maria-style barbecue pit is available. Contact the Ventura County General Services Agency for fees and reservations.

Die-hard, back-country riders will probably find the Ojai Valley Trail too civilized and noisy, but for families with small children, it's a safe and pleasant place to enjoy an outing.

Pacific Crest Trail

The Pacific Crest National Scenic Trail (PCT) extends 2,638 miles and connects Mexico and Canada through California, Oregon, and Washington. Formally completed in 1993, the trail winds through desert chaparral, alpine meadows, and glaciated granite. It passes through twenty-four national forests, seven national parks, thirty-three wilderness areas, six state/province parks, and four Bureau of Land Management areas. The advocacy group for the PCT is the Pacific Crest Trail Association, a public membership association that sponsors trail maintenance crews for the PCT and feeder trails.

Dr. Ben York, President of the Pacific Crest Trail Association, is one of the few people who has ridden the entire trail:

> It was sometime in October 1991 when I mentioned to [my wife] Adeline that I would like to ride the PCT in two-week increments per year. She responded by saying, "By the time you get two weeks in, you are just getting settled into the routine, so let's do it all." She didn't realize that it was a 2,638-mile trail.
>
> I guess every night I dream about the whole experience. It was such a great adventure—the wonderful opportunity to see the spectacular scenes. I am often asked what spot I liked the most. I cannot answer, for each scene has its own unique beauty and character. The same has to be said for every person that I met along the way.
>
> From *PCT by 2 in 1992* by Ben and Adeline York

For more information about the Pacific Crest Trail Association, write to 5325 Elkhorn Blvd. #256, Sacramento CA 95842, or call (800) 817-2243, Monday through Friday, 9 A.M. to 6 P.M.

Although the PCT traverses several areas listed in this guide, two staging locations, Boulder Oaks Campground (pages 104–109) and Kamp-Anza Kampground (pages 110–115), focus on PCT access. A description of each follows.

Pacific Crest Trail
Boulder Oaks Campground

Contributed by Betty Swift

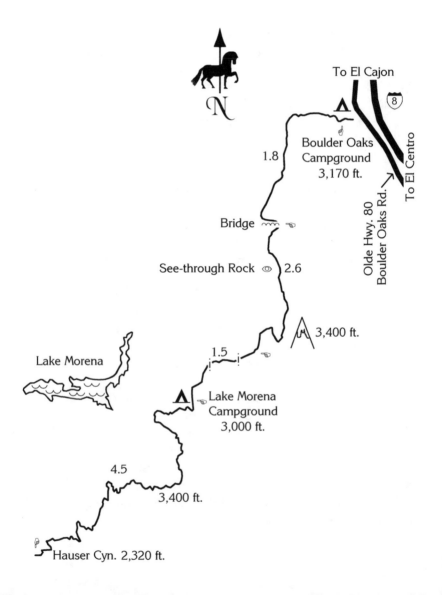

To El Cajon

Boulder Oaks
Campground
3,170 ft.

1.8

Olde Hwy. 80
Boulder Oaks Rd.

To El Centro

Bridge

See-through Rock   2.6

3,400 ft.

1.5

Lake Morena

Lake Morena
Campground
3,000 ft.

4.5

3,400 ft.

Hauser Cyn. 2,320 ft.

Pacific Crest Trail
Boulder Oaks Campground

Contributed by Betty Swift

Located near the town of Boulder Oaks, approximately 45 miles east of San Diego off Interstate 8. For additional information and reservations, contact the Cleveland National Forest, Descanso Ranger District, 3348 Alpine Boulevard, Alpine CA 91901, (619) 445-6235, Monday through Friday, 8 A.M. to 4:30 P.M., fax (619) 445-1753. Make reservations at least 10 days in advance with the National Forest Reservation Center, (800) 280-2267, Monday through Friday, 8:30 A.M. to 10:30 P.M., Saturday and Sunday, 11 A.M. to 7 P.M.

Hours
        Day Use .... Sunrise to Sunset
        Overnight .... Check-out 2 P.M.
Fee
        Day Use .... None
        Overnight .... $16/night, includes two 12-by-12-foot pipe corrals.
Getting There .... U
Parking .... U
Hitching Rails/Corrals .... No/Yes
Trail Difficulty
        Physical Ability .... U U to U U U
        Training Level .... U U to U U U
Elevation
        Boulder Oaks Campground .... 3,170 feet
        Highest Point .... 3,400 feet
        Hauser Canyon .... 2,320 feet
Water
        Camp .... People: Yes Horse: Yes
        Trail .... People: No Horse: Seasonal
Toilets .... Yes, pit

Directions:

Exit Interstate 8 at Buckman Springs Road and go south .1 miles to Olde Highway 80 (Boulder Oaks Road). Turn left onto Olde Highway 80 and travel 2.1 miles to the campground; turn right.

Description:

Developed in 1985 with the help of many volunteers, Boulder Oaks Campground is the perfect place to begin a ride on the Pacific Crest Trail.

Day-use parking is available or plan to stay overnight. Nestled among boulders, sagebrush, and oak trees, you'll find seventeen pull-through campsites, most with tables and stoves. Piped water is available, but bring a very long hose or carry buckets for your horses. The Forest Service suggests you bring padlocks for each corral and use them whenever your horses are stabled.

To begin your ride, head south out of the campground until you reach a horse gate. After closing the gate behind you, turn west on a well-marked trail through chaparral, scrub oaks, and an occasional red shank chamise. There is one seasonal water crossing in the first .5 miles with an easy slope into and out of it. The next section of trail has clear signs or is well marked. Continue over a small hill where you'll encounter a few rocky spots; then head down into a meadow with grazing cows and calves. Please stay on the trail because you are crossing private land, and the owner is very particular about people going off the trail.

Now there will be a couple of gullies to negotiate before paralleling an old road. Follow the road for a short distance to the bridge across Cottonwood Creek. Cross the creek and continue along the north side of the bridge to the last arch on the east; then turn south under the bridge and pick up the trail again.

After the bridge, turn left and begin to climb up several switchbacks. The trail becomes more difficult at this point, with rocky parts and a 75-foot-long narrow section with a rocky drop-off on the right. The highest point—3,400 feet—provides panoramic views of Lake Morena and the surrounding area. You'll then wind back down to the 3,000-foot level and go through a pretty canyon lined with oak trees, lilac, manzanita, and many interesting boulders. From here, the PCT continues to the Lake Morena County Park and Hauser Canyon, or you can explore one of several side trails before returning to Boulder Oaks Campground via the way you came (it's not possible to make a loop back to the campground because of the willow growth in Cottonwood Creek).

If you wish to explore Hauser Canyon, continue south from the Lake Morena County Park on the PCT. The next 4.5-mile section of trail to Hauser Canyon is the hardest. It climbs the southern slopes of Morena Butte for approximately 1,400 feet via switchbacks and through some rocky spots, but the views are spectacular. After reaching an old road that you follow for about 75 feet, the trail takes off to the left for about a mile through boulders and chaparral. Then you'll have a long downhill stretch of approximately 2 miles into Hauser Canyon. This is a narrow switchback trail along the side of the mountain. Once in the canyon, there is an old road that can be explored. As you continue down the canyon, the creek crossings become more rocky and deep due to water escaping from Lake Morena. Rattlesnakes are a definite hazard, so do keep an eye out for them and carry first aid in case of a bite. Summer temperatures can exceed 100 degrees. Consider a spring or winter ride to avoid the worst heat—and remember to carry plenty of water and drink it.

The Pacific Crest National Scenic Trail is a national treasure located right in our own backyard. Hopefully, the ride from Hauser Canyon and Boulder Oaks Campground will inspire you to explore other sections between here and Canada.

Desert Willow
(Chilopsis linearis)

Pacific Crest Trail
Staging at Kamp-Anza Kampground
Access from Coyote Canyon/Anza-Borrego Desert
State Park

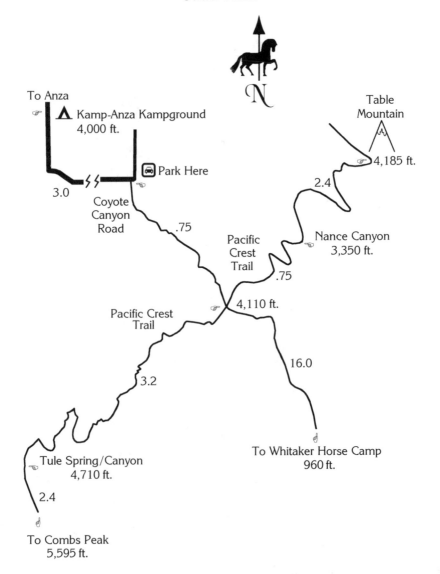

N

To Anza

Kamp-Anza Kampground
4,000 ft.

Park Here

Table
Mountain

4,185 ft.

3.0

2.4

Coyote
Canyon
Road

.75

Pacific
Crest
Trail

Nance Canyon
3,350 ft.

.75

Pacific Crest
Trail

4,110 ft.

16.0

3.2

Tule Spring/Canyon
4,710 ft.

To Whitaker Horse Camp
960 ft.

2.4

To Combs Peak
5,595 ft.

Pacific Crest Trail
Staging at Kamp-Anza Kampground
Access from Coyote Canyon/Anza-Borrego Desert
State Park

Located east of Temecula and southwest of Indio in the town of Anza. For maps and additional information about Kamp-Anza, contact Terry Grant, Kamp-Anza Kampground, 41560 Terwilliger Road, Anza CA 92539, (909) 763-4819, daily, 7:30 A.M. to 7 P.M.

For maps and information about Coyote Canyon and Vernon V. Whitaker Horse Camp contact the Anza-Borrego Desert State Park, P.O. Box 299, Borrego Springs CA 92004, (619) 767-5311, Monday through Friday, 8 A.M. to 5 P.M. (The 619 area code will change to 760 on March 22, 1997.)

Hours	None
Fee	$12.50/night includes one horse. Additional horses are $5.00/night each.
Getting There	♘♘
Parking	♘
Hitching Rails/Corrals	Yes/Yes
Trail Difficulty	
Physical Ability	♘♘ to ♘♘♘♘
Training Level	♘ to ♘♘♘
Elevation	
Kamp-Anza	4,000 feet
PCT at Coyote Canyon	4,110 feet
Water	
Camp	People: Yes Horse: Yes
Trail	People: No Horse: Seasonal
Toilets	Yes, flush
OHVs	Yes, (Coyote Canyon)

Directions:

Take Interstate 15 to Temecula; exit at State Highway 79 south. Travel 17.6 miles to Aguanga and turn left onto State Highway 371. Continue 16.4 miles into the town of Anza and turn right on Kirby Road. Travel 3.3 miles and turn left into Kamp-Anza Kampground. (Kirby Road doglegs twice, becoming Terwilliger Road.)

Description:

Staging at Kamp-Anza Kampground allows you to explore two excellent trails: the Pacific Crest Trail and Coyote Canyon, which leads south to Vernon V. Whitaker Horse Camp in the Anza-Borrego Desert State Park. Those who don't want to spend the night at Kamp-Anza can park at the intersection of Coyote Canyon Road and Yucca Valley Road and ride from there. This is also an option for Kamp-Anza campers who want to eliminate the 3-mile ride from the campground to the trailhead and back again.

The PCT crosses Coyote Canyon approximately 1 mile from the intersection of Yucca Valley Road. Turning left (northeast) onto the PCT, you'll head down a well-marked trail into Nance Canyon where cottonwood and water-loving grasses cling to sandy ribbons on either side of a small stream. This land is rich with color: green, red, and yellow lichen-covered rocks line the trail, as does buckwheat (creamy white in the spring, a rich brick-red in the fall), mountain laurel, manzanita, and cholo cactus. Keep the pliers or hemostats handy to remove cactus spines from your horse's legs.

From the bottom of Nance Canyon, the trail climbs the shoulder of Table Mountain, offering spectacular views of Anza-Borrego Desert State Park and possibly some desert bighorn sheep (*Borrego cimarron*) that inhabit the area.

If you turn right from Coyote Canyon onto the PCT, you'll ride through undulating rock ravines and sandy hillsides, covered with ribbonwood and chamise, toward Tule Spring. This is probably best ridden by horses and riders in moderate-to-excellent condition.

Coyote Canyon Road is a wide, smooth dirt road leading to Vernon V. Whitaker Horse Camp, which is approximately 17 miles south. If you are adventurous, well conditioned, and have someone who can shuttle your rig to Whitaker Horse Camp, consider a one-way ride down the canyon. Pack plenty of water for yourself—and drink it. There should be several places along Coyote Creek where your horse can water, but verify conditions with Anza-Borrego Park Rangers before starting out.

The facilities at Whitaker Horse Camp are plush—solar showers, flush toilets, and good corrals—and you'll have plenty to talk about as you gather around a crackling campfire to roast marshmallows. For more information about the camp, see *Horseback Riding Trails of Southern California Volume I* or contact the Anza-Borrego Desert State Park Headquarters at the address listed above.

When you ride in the desert, always carry plenty of water. Wear sunscreen, a hat, and sunglasses. Recorded temperatures in Anza-Borrego Desert State Park have changed as much as 80 degrees during a 24-hour period, so bring appropriate clothing. Insect repellent is a good idea, too. Give a wide berth to snakes and scorpions—they will usually get out of your way if you let them. Mountain lions also make their home in the park. Coyote Canyon is closed from June 15 through September 15 when the desert bighorn sheep mate and give birth in the canyon.

Kamp-Anza Kampground is a private facility owned by Terry and Marilynn Grant and offers many amenities to equestrians: pipe corrals for approximately twenty horses, some hitching rails, water at each corral, hot showers, flush toilets with electrical outlets, laundry facilities, spa, telephones, and a general store. You can park most anywhere in the 10-acre equestrian camping area, although tent campers will probably want to pitch their tent on a small, grassy circle shaded by cottonwood and pine trees. You'll need to clean your own corral, but Kamp-Anza provides a wheelbarrow and dumpster.

Kamp-Anza is listed in several PCT trail guides as a resupply stop for travelers on the PCT, so you might have the opportunity to swap stories with one of these hearty souls.

Spring, fall, and winter are the best times to explore Coyote Canyon and the PCT. During a 2- to 3-week period in March or April, desert wildflowers erupt in a riot of color. For more information, contact the Anza-Borrego Desert State Park wildflower hotline at (619) 767-4684. (The area code for this number will change to 760 on March 22, 1997.)

Red Box
National Forest Road 2N24
Gabrielino National Recreation Trail

To the Antelope Valley

To La Cañada Flintridge

Shortcut Picnic Area
4,696 ft.

To Charlton Flats

Angeles
Crest Hwy.

Valley Forge
3,500 ft.

3.3

SMT

SMT
Silver Moccasin Trail

Red Box→
4,660 ft.

3.0

2.0

WFC

WFC
West Fork
Campground
3,100 ft.

Mt. Wilson
Road

5.3

To Tumbler

Mt. Wilson

Spruce Grove
3,100 ft.

Red Box
National Forest Road 2N24
Gabrielino National Recreation Trail

Located in the Angeles National Forest north of Altadena, south of the Antelope Valley. For additional information and maps, contact the U.S. Forest Service, Arroyo Seco Ranger District, Oak Grove Park, Flintridge CA 91011, (818) 790-1151, Monday through Friday, 8 A.M. to 4:30 P.M.

Hours	Sunrise to Sunset
Fee	None
Getting There	🐎🐎 to 🐎🐎🐎
Parking	🐎🐎
Hitching Rails/Corrals	Yes/Yes (four, day-use-only corrals)

Trail Difficulty

Physical Ability	🐎🐎 to 🐎🐎🐎🐎
Training Level	🐎🐎 to 🐎🐎🐎

Elevation

Red Box	4,660 feet
Valley Forge Campground	3,500 feet
West Fork Campground	3,100 feet

Water

Staging Area	People: Yes Horse: Yes
Trail	People: No Horse: Seasonal
Toilets	Yes, flush

Directions:

From the Antelope Valley and North: Take State Highway 14, the Antelope Valley Freeway, south to Acton. Exit at Angeles Forest Highway and turn right onto Sierra Highway. Make an immediate left (south) onto Angeles Forest Highway. From Santa Clarita and West: Take State Highway 14, the Antelope Valley Freeway, north to Acton. Exit at Angeles Forest Highway and continue straight ahead, across Sierra Highway, onto Angeles Forest Highway.

<u>Both:</u> From Angeles Forest Highway and Sierra Highway, travel 17.2 miles to Upper Big Tujunga Canyon Road and turn left. Continue 9.9 miles to State Highway 2, the Angeles Crest Highway; turn right. Go 4.6 miles and turn left onto Mount Wilson Road. Make an immediate left into the Red Box parking lot.

<u>From the San Fernando Valley and South:</u> Take Interstate 210, the Foothill Freeway, to La Cañada Flintridge; exit at State Highway 2, the Angeles Crest Highway, and go north. Continue 14.8 miles to Mount Wilson Road and turn right. Make an immediate left into the Red Box parking lot.

Description:

Nestled in the heart of the Angeles National Forest, Red Box is an easy-to-access starting point for those who want to experience the rugged beauty and cobalt skies of the nation's second national forest. (The first was the Yellowstone Park Timberland Reserve, established in 1891 and later renamed Yellowstone National Park.)

Though clearly designed as a horsemen's staging area, the Red Box parking area is less than ideal. It's paved—right up to the gates of the four corrals. Since camping is not allowed, the corrals are rarely used and in need of some repair. Water is available, but you'll have to carry buckets for your horses. The parking lot will accommodate two or three truck-trailer rigs but only if you arrive early and take up several single-vehicle parking spaces. When parking your rig, be considerate of other users who need a place to park. And do remember to bring a rake and clean up after your horses. Garbage cans and two picnic tables are provided, and flush toilets are available across Mount Wilson Road at the ranger station.

In between the day-use corrals and Mount Wilson Road is a gated dirt road—2N24. Begin your ride here. Riders looking for a challenge should look for a narrow trail on the left (before reaching the gate) and head down the canyon on the Gabrielino National Recreation Trail. You'll have to push through dense chaparral and scurry over sharp rocks as you negotiate several hairpin switchbacks, but the ride offers splendid views of the canyon—the major watershed of the West Fork of the San Gabriel River.

The alternative is a more relaxing ride down 2N24, a dirt road that roughly parallels the Gabrielino Trail and provides Forest Service vehicle access to Valley Forge and West Fork Campgrounds. The locked gate prevents public vehicle access, so you'll have to squeeze between the gatepost and a tree—a mere 23 inches wide— to get on the road.

Pines, sycamore, scrub oak, and manzanita grow on the rugged hillsides, and yellow-flowering broom, yucca, and chamise offer spring and summer color. Many years ago, the Shoshone Indians traveled the canyon, collecting yucca fibers for nets and ropes, and manzanita berries for cider.

Ronald W. Caspers Wilderness Park

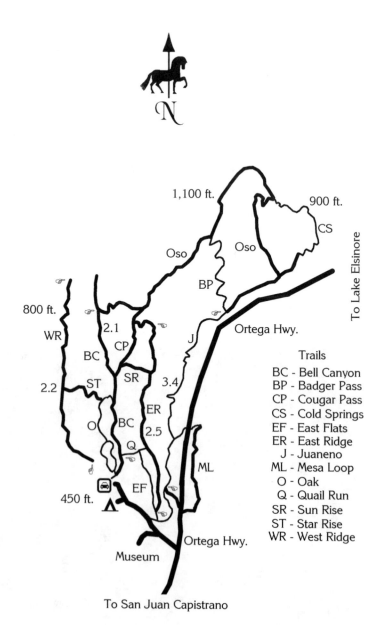

N

1,100 ft.

900 ft.

CS

Oso

Oso

BP

800 ft.

To Lake Elsinore

WR

2.1

Ortega Hwy.

CP

J

BC

SR

3.4

2.2

ST

ER

O

BC

2.5

Q

ML

EF

450 ft.

Ortega Hwy.

Museum

To San Juan Capistrano

Trails

BC - Bell Canyon
BP - Badger Pass
CP - Cougar Pass
CS - Cold Springs
EF - East Flats
ER - East Ridge
J - Juaneno
ML - Mesa Loop
O - Oak
Q - Quail Run
SR - Sun Rise
ST - Star Rise
WR - West Ridge

Ronald W. Caspers Wilderness Park

A 7,600-acre wilderness park located 7.5 miles east of San Juan Capistrano in the foothills of the Santa Ana Mountains. For additional information, reservations, and maps, contact the Ronald W. Caspers Wilderness Park, 33401 Ortega Highway, P.O. Box 395, San Juan Capistrano CA 92675-0395, (714) 728-0235, Monday through Friday, 8 A.M. to 4:30 P.M.

Hours
- Day Use .... 7 A.M. to Sunset
- Overnight .... Check-out 2 P.M.

Fee
- Day Use $2/horse
- Overnight .... $10/night plus $2/horse. Each site has two 12-by-12-foot corrals.

Getting There .... 🐴

Parking .... 🐴

Hitching Rails/Corrals .... Yes/Yes

Trail Difficulty
- Physical Ability.. 🐴 to 🐴🐴🐴
- Training Level.. 🐴 to 🐴🐴🐴

Elevation
- Camp .... 450 feet
- West Ridge Trail .... 800 feet
- Oso Trail .... 1,100 feet (approximately)

Water
- Camp .... People: Yes Horse: Yes
- Trail .... People: No Horse: Seasonal

Toilets .... Yes, pit

Bicycles .... Yes, 🚴 (on dirt roads only)

Directions:

Take Interstate 5 to San Juan Capistrano. Exit at State Highway 74, the Ortega Highway, and travel east 7.5 miles. Turn left into the park.

Description:

Once the crown jewel in Orange County's regional park system, Caspers was closed after two separate mountain lion attacks in 1986. The park was reopened in 1995 when a judge ruled that governmental bodies are not liable for the actions of wildlife. However, minors are not allowed beyond the campgrounds unless accompanied by a trained docent or ranger, and they must be under direct adult supervision at all times while in the campgrounds. If you have minors who want to explore the trails, call the park and explain your situation; they'll arrange for a mounted guide. All visitors must obtain a Wilderness Use Permit from the entrance booth. No pets, except horses, are allowed.

All that said, with 30 miles of trails that traverse chaparral-covered hillsides, rock-strewn riverbeds, and oak- and sycamore-shaded groves, Caspers Wilderness Park is a first-rate riding destination. The camping facilities make it an excellent choice for a weekend (or longer) outing.

Star Mesa Equestrian Campground has thirty pull-through sites, each with two 12-by-12-foot pipe corrals. A picnic table, fire stove, and hitching rail are provided at each site. Water bibs are plentiful but somehow manage to be a long way from the corrals. Bring at least 50 feet of hose or plan to carry buckets of water. You'll also need a rake to move manure from the corrals to the aisle where park personnel will scoop it up with a tractor for disposal. Many of the sites are nestled under gnarled old sycamore trees, which provide welcome summer shade. The two pit toilets are not quite enough to service a full campground, but additional facilities are available at Live Oak Grove Campground, Owl and Quail Group Area, and the Old Corral Equestrian Day Use Area.

Groups must make advanced reservations. Individuals may make reservations but will be charged a hefty, nonrefundable reservation fee in addition to the camping fees. Most individuals call ahead to find out if a group is booked, then camp on a first-come, first-served basis. Park management occasionally designates the Old Corral for overflow camping.

An excellent place to begin your exploration of Caspers is the Oak Trail, a wide, mostly flat path. As you ride through great stands of sycamores and coast live oaks, your horse's hoofbeats are muted by the soft dirt and decaying leaves. Cactus wren and the ever-noisy scrub jays flit from tree to tree. Mule deer hide in the late afternoon shadows, stepping into sun-gilded meadows to graze when they think you aren't looking. Take a deep breath and leave a hectic workweek behind.

Spring rains bring poppies, chia, and other wildflowers, and when the San Juan Creek flows, you might spot the spectacular great blue heron (*Ardea herodias*). Hard to miss, these crane-like birds are blue-gray with a 6-foot wingspan.

For a more energetic ride with panoramic views, including the Pacific Ocean, try the West Ridge Trail that follows the mountain spine along the west edge of the park. From here you might spot a red-tailed or Cooper's hawk riding the updrafts.

Another easy ride, the Bell Canyon Trail, follows a streamside habitat that includes plants such as cattails, ferns, and watercress. Bell Canyon is so named because, according to legend, when local Indians struck a particular boulder, it made a bell-ringing sound that echoed through the canyon.

Folks who live near Caspers are fortunate to have this beautiful park so close at hand. For those who must travel to get there, Caspers is a pleasant overnight destination that you'll want to visit again and again.

Miner's Lettuce
(Claytonia perfoliata)

L. EBERT '96

Saddleback Butte State Park

N

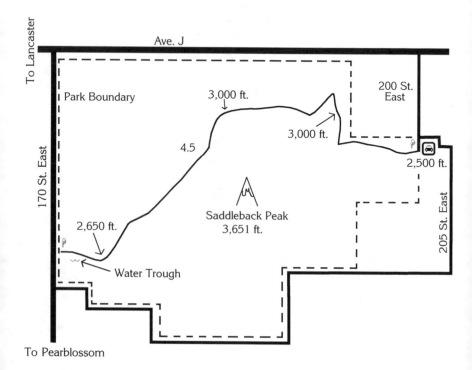

Saddleback Butte State Park

A 2,955-acre state park located 22 miles east of Lancaster in the Antelope Valley. For a horse trail permit, gate combination, map, and additional information, contact California State Parks, Mojave Desert Sector, 1051 West Avenue M #201, Lancaster CA 93534, (805) 942-0662, Monday through Friday, 8 A.M. to 4:30 P.M.

Hours	Sunrise to Sunset
Fee	$1/person
Getting There	♘
Parking	♘
Hitching Rails/Corrals	No/No
Trail Difficulty	
Physical Ability	♘
Training Level	♘
Elevation	2,500 feet
Water	
Staging Area	People: No Horse: No
Trail	People: No Horse: Water trough at west end of trail but is not always filled.
Toilets	No

Directions:

Take State Highway 14, the Antelope Valley Freeway, to Lancaster. If traveling north, exit at 20th Street West and turn right. Go .6 miles to Avenue J and turn right (east). If traveling south, exit at Avenue J and go east. From Avenue J, continue east for 22.2 miles to 200th Street East and turn right (south) onto the dirt road (it's easy to miss). Continue .5 miles to the locked entrance gate to the parking area.

Description:

Newly developed in conjunction with the Antelope Valley Trails, Recreation, and Environmental Council, the 4.5-mile horse trail is an easy ride that skirts the lower north and west portions of the butte. The trail is outlined by a fence and rock border, and horses must be kept on the trail and in the designated staging area. A water trough is located on the west end of the trail, though it isn't always filled. To make an 11-mile loop, exit the park past the water trough and turn left. Follow the dirt trails that parallel the park boundary fence and circle back to 205th Street East.

Saddleback Butte is a deeply weathered, granite mountain top that rises some 1,000 feet above the alluvial bottom land that we call the Antelope Valley. Although composed mostly of light-colored quartz and feldspar minerals, parts of the butte are coated with dark manganese oxide, sometimes called desert varnish. It's a quiet place where individual sounds are easy to identify and the air has been scoured clean by sand and sage. Creosote bush is the predominant plant here. In the spring, the sparse foliage is covered with pea-sized, yellow flowers and tiny white puff-balls of seed. Closer to the ground, the sharp-eyed observer will find a variety of wildflowers such as the lavender, sunflower-shaped desert aster, and mats of tiny, sweet-smelling yellow coreopsis. The desert dandelion, primrose, and sunflower families are also well represented.

Of the many animals that live in the park, the desert tortoise is perhaps the most well known. Turtles and tortoises are ancient life forms, dating back 200 million years—earlier than even the first dinosaurs. The desert tortoise burrows in the sand to escape summer's broiling heat and winter's cold and can travel up to 20 feet per minute unless sidetracked by a tasty-looking plant.

In order to ride the buttes, you'll need to plan ahead. First, contact the California State Park office at the phone number listed above and obtain a Saddleback Butte State Park Horse Trail Permit. If you live near Lancaster, you can stop by the office during open hours. Return the filled-out permit with your fee to the Lancaster office. Upon receipt, you will receive the gate combination and can then go to the park.

Saddleback Butte State Park is best enjoyed either in the spring when great swaths of the Antelope Valley are painted orange with California poppies or during the fall and winter after the summer heat has dissipated.

Thorn Meadows Campground
Fishbowls

Contributed by Jennifer and Rick Fuller

𝒩

To Reyes Creek   Lockwood Valley Rd.   To Lake of the Woods
and Frazier Park

7N03
Grade Valley Rd.
a.k.a. Thorn Mdw. Rd.

Pine Spring
Campground
5,900 ft.

To Stone
House
4,600 ft.

21W05

8.0

Fishbowls
5,070 ft.

Halfmoon

To Bear Trap #1

3.0

4.0

4.0

Haddock 6,230 ft.

3.0

Mutau Flat
4,925 ft.

5.0

3.0

Thorn Meadows
Campground
5,250 ft.

Pine Mtn.
Lodge
6,050 ft.

Thorn
Point
6,935 ft.

To Lion Campground
and State Hwy. 33

Thorn Meadows Campground
Fishbowls

Contributed by Jennifer and Rick Fuller

Located southeast of Mount Piños in the Los Padres National Forest. For maps and additional information, contact the Mount Piños Ranger District Office, HC 1 Box 400, 34580 Lockwood Valley Road, Frazier Park CA 93225, (805) 245-3731, Monday through Saturday, 8 A.M. to 4:30 P.M.

Hours	None
Fee	None
Getting There	U
Parking	U U
Hitching Rails/Corrals	No/Yes
Trail Difficulty	
Physical Ability	U U to U U U U
Training Level	U U to U U U
Elevation	5,250 feet
Water	
Camp	People: No Horse: No
Trail	People: No Horse: Creek
Toilets	Yes, pit

Directions:

From Los Angeles: Take Interstate 5 north to the Frazier Park exit and turn left (west). (From Bakersfield: Take Interstate 5 south to the Frazier Park exit and turn right.) Travel 6.5 miles to Lockwood Valley Road and turn left. Continue 10 miles to Grade Valley Road (a.k.a. Thorn Meadows Road) and turn left (the brown Forest Service sign indicates Mutau Flats). Continue 6.5 miles on the dirt road to Thorn Meadows Campground.

Description:

If you're looking to escape summer's triple-digit temperatures, pack a bathing suit and head for Thorn Meadows Campground. Situated at 5,250 feet and surrounded by vanilla-scented Jeffrey pines, it's a lovely staging point for a 7-mile ride to the Fishbowls. The Fishbowls' deep pools, carved out of solid rock, are a popular summer swimming spot and have been known to contain trout. Incense cedars grow among the pine trees, and in the spring, many wildflowers color the meadows. From Fishbowls, you can loop back to the campground, making a 15-mile round trip, or head back the way you came and explore the trail to Pine Mountain Lodge and beyond.

The trail is wide and well marked but can be dusty in places, which makes a dip in the Fishbowls all the more inviting. You'll cross several creeks where your horse can drink, but do carry water for yourself.

Thorn Meadows Campground is a first-come, first-served campground with five sites and a public corral. If you plan to spend the night, you might want to bring a portable corral in case the public corral is being used. The Forest Service refers to Thorn Meadows as a pack-it-in, pack-it-out campground, which means no garbage cans. You'll have to collect your horse's manure in plastic bags and dispose of it elsewhere along with your trash. Picnic tables and fire rings are provided. The entire area closes after the first snow, so check conditions with the ranger station if you plan to ride here in early winter or early spring.

For folks who live in northern Los Angeles County, Thorn Meadows is the perfect quick getaway riding destination. For out-of-area visitors, this section of the Los Padres National Forest is worth exploring.

Photo by Jennifer Fuller

Upper Oso Campground
Santa Cruz Trail

N

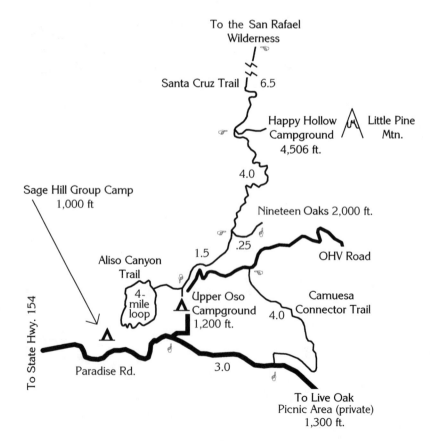

To the San Rafael
Wilderness

Santa Cruz Trail   6.5

Happy Hollow   Little Pine
Campground   Mtn.
4,506 ft.

4.0

Sage Hill Group Camp
1,000 ft.

Nineteen Oaks 2,000 ft.

1.5   .25   OHV Road

Aliso Canyon
Trail

4-   Upper Oso   Camuesa
mile   Campground   Connector Trail
loop   1,200 ft.   4.0

Paradise Rd.   3.0

To Live Oak
Picnic Area (private)
1,300 ft.

To State Hwy. 154

Upper Oso Campground
Santa Cruz Trail

Located in the Santa Ynez Recreation Area of the Los Padres National Forest, north of Santa Barbara and southeast of Lake Cachuma* off State Highway 154. For detailed maps and additional information, contact the Los Padres National Forest, Los Prietos Ranger Station, Star Route, Santa Barbara CA 93105, (805) 967-3481, Monday through Saturday, 8 A.M. to 5 P.M. For reservations, call the National Forest Reservation Center, (800) 280-2267, Monday through Friday, 8:30 A.M. to 10:30 P.M., Saturday and Sunday, 11 A.M. to 7 P.M. (*See page 37 for information about the Cachuma Lake Equestrian Trail.)

Hours
    Day Use .... 6 A.M. to 8 P.M.
    Overnight .... Check-in 2 P.M.
Fee
    Day Use .... None
    Overnight $8/night
Getting There .... U U
Parking .... U to U U
Hitching Rails/Corrals .... No/Yes
Trail Difficulty
    Physical Ability .... U U to U U U U
    Training Level .... U U to U U U
Elevation
    Upper Oso Campground .... 1,200 feet
    Happy Hollow/Little Pine Mtn. .... 4,506 feet
Water
    Camp .... People: Yes Horse: Yes
    Trail .... People: No Horse: Seasonal
Toilets .... Yes, yes
OHVs .... Yes, 🏁 (in day-use area
                                               and on designated route)

Directions:

From Santa Barbara: Take U.S. 101 to Santa Barbara, exit at State Highway 154, and go north. Travel 10.6 miles to Paradise Road and turn right.

From the Santa Ynez/Solvang Area: From U.S. 101, take State Highway 154 south 21.3 miles to Paradise Road. Turn left.

Both: Continue 5.7 miles. You'll ford the Santa Ynez River and arrive in Lower Oso Picnic Area. Turn left at the sign to Upper Oso Campground and continue 1 mile on a one-lane paved road into camp.

Description:

One of Santa Barbara's better kept secrets is Upper Oso Campground. Each of the thirteen equestrian campsites is situated near a gigantic oak tree, so the spreading branches shade the campsite and/or corral. In the spring, a carpet of wild oats makes for a nice after-ride snack for your horse (and a soft spot to spread out your blanket for a nap!). Piped water is available at central locations throughout the campground. You'll have to carry buckets for your horses. Each site comes with a concrete table, fire pit, stove, and one 24-by-24-foot, six-rail pipe corral. Extra corrals are not available. You are responsible for collecting your horse's manure and getting it to the dumpsters.

As night's purple hues melt into the canyon, a colony of frogs living along Oso Creek begins to sing. Look for deer nibbling on tender greenery along the outer edges of the camp. Other nighttime animals to watch for include owls and possums.

Upper Oso offers access to the popular Santa Cruz Trail. The trail begins at the north end of camp and follows Oso Creek for 2 miles. (Make sure you get on the trail and not the off-highway vehicle road that parallels the creek.) You'll cross the rock-strewn creek a dozen times or more—a good opportunity to improve your horse's water negotiating skills—as you meander through the narrow sandstone canyon, which is shaded by sycamores and oaks. Bring bug repellent, as mosquitos and gnats can be a problem. Spring flowers are abundant, including virgin's bower, monkey flower, and several varieties of little purple flowers that require a botanist to identify them. And watch out for poison oak.

At a signed junction, you can take a spur to Nineteen Oaks, situated on a knoll overlooking Oso Canyon. On these drier slopes, look for mariposa lillies, paintbrush, blue dicks, and even a field of poppies. Nineteen Oaks has a couple of shaded picnic tables that make a pleasant snack or lunch stop.

At the Nineteen Oaks junction, you leave behind the cool, shaded Oso Creek and begin a relentless 3.5-mile climb to Little Pine Mountain. The trail is rocky, very narrow in parts, and best suited for the well-conditioned horse and rider. There is no water along the way, but you'll get spectacular views of the Santa Ynez River Valley.

After the long climb, you and your horse will appreciate a rest under a canopy of Jeffrey pines and black oaks at Happy Hollow Campround at the top of Little Pine Mountain. From there, the Santa Cruz Trail continues north another 6.5 miles to the San Rafael Wilderness. Contact the ranger station for information and required permits for wilderness travel.

Walnut Creek Park Trail

Contributed by Joan Phelan

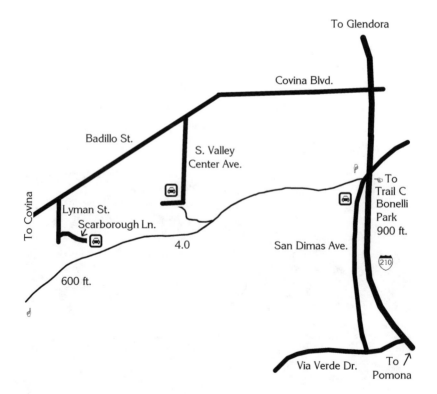

To Glendora

Covina Blvd.

Badillo St.

S. Valley
Center Ave.

To Covina

Lyman St.
Scarborough Ln.

4.0

600 ft.

To
Trail C
Bonelli
Park
900 ft.

San Dimas Ave.

210

Via Verde Dr.

To
Pomona

WALNUT CREEK PARK TRAIL

CONTRIBUTED by JOAN PHELAN

A 4-mile trail connecting to Trail C in the Frank G. Bonelli Regional County Park (see page 53). The Walnut Creek Park Trail is located in west San Dimas. For additional information and maps, contact Jim Campos at (818) 575-5756, Monday through Thursday and alternate Fridays, 6:30 A.M. to 3:30 P.M., or Bertha Ruiz at the Los Angeles County Department of Parks and Recreation, 433 S. Vermont Avenue, Los Angeles CA 90020, (213) 738-2973, Monday through Thursday, 6:30 A.M. to 5:30 P.M.

Hours	Sunrise to Sunset
Fee	None
Getting There	U
Parking	U U
Hitching Rails/Corrals	Yes/No
Trail Difficulty	
Physical Ability	U
Training Level	U U
Elevation	
Lyman Staging Area	600 feet
San Dimas Staging Area	900 feet
Water	
Staging Area	People: No Horse: No
Trail	People: No Horse: Creek
Toilets	Yes, pit at the S. Valley Center Parking Area
Bicyclists	Yes, (occasional)

Directions:

To the Lyman Staging Area: From Interstate 210, exit at Covina Boulevard and go west (left). After .9 miles, Covina Boulevard turns into Badillo Street. Continue on Badillo Street for another 1 mile and then turn left (south) on Lyman Street. Continue .2 miles; then turn left onto Scarborough Lane (east). Continue .2 miles into the parking area.

To the S. Valley Center Staging Area: From Interstate 210, exit at Covina Boulevard and go west (left). After .9 miles, Covina Boulevard turns into Badillo Street. Continue on Badillo Street .2 miles to S. Valley Center Avenue. Turn left on S. Valley Center Avenue and go .5 miles to the end of the road. Park along the west side of S. Valley Center Avenue or make a right on Gainsborough Road and park on the south side.

To the San Dimas Staging Area: From Interstate 210, exit at Via Verde Drive and turn east (right). Travel .1 miles and turn right onto San Dimas Avenue. Continue 1 mile. The staging area is a dirt pullout on your left.

Description:

When the heat of summer leaves you longing for a hammock, consider an escape to the Walnut Creek Park Trail. Approximately 80 percent of the trail meanders through stands of oak, pine, eucalyptus, and sycamore—some over 100 feet tall. You can picnic along the way, resting under a canopy of leaves that filters heat and sun like a gauze umbrella. Lined with wild blackberries and ferns, Walnut Creek gurgles close-by. Where the water slows, waterbugs dot the surface. You might even find some tadpoles hiding in wispy strands of algae. A variety of birds make their home in this microcommunity, including egrets, great blue herons, and kingfishers.

You can stage at one of three areas: Lyman, S. Valley Center, or San Dimas. The Lyman staging area (which is really at the end of Scarborough Lane) can accommodate several rigs if folks are considerate about how they park. Remember to leave room for others to get in—and out. Staging at S. Valley Center is along a paved street and can handle several rigs. The residents will appreciate it if you pack a rake and clean up after your horses. The San Dimas staging area is little more than a dirt pullout and will accommodate only two or three rigs.

Photo by Joan Phelan

Walnut Creek Park Trail is wide and mostly flat with many creek crossings—perfect for introducing a young horse to water. Winter rains can turn the creek into a raging torrent and make the trail and some staging areas unusable, so check with the Department of Parks and Recreation if you plan to ride after a rain.

Spring brings many wildflowers, including blue fern-leaf phacelia and monkey flower. Keep an eye out for poison oak—it grows well in the moist soil and frequently intertwines with blackberry bushes.

For folks looking for a peaceful place to ride, the Walnut Creek Park Trail is a nifty little piece of heaven.

GENERAL EQUIPMENT AND SUPPLIES

- Wear protective clothing including gloves, hat, and sturdy boots or riding tennis shoes. Protective head gear is available in western hat styles. See page 150 for sources.
- Sunglasses, sunscreen, insect repellent, and lip protection. A bandanna will keep the sun off your neck.
- Water. Allow 1 gallon per person per day. Allow at least 10 gallons per horse. You can purchase collapsible 5-gallon containers from a camping or sporting goods store.
- A map of the area and this guidebook
- Pocket knife
- Wire cutters
- Hoof pick (carry in saddlebags)
- First-aid kit for both horse and rider
- Spare halter and lead rope
- Buckets for water. Consider carrying a folding bucket in your saddlebag to use when water is available but not convenient to approach with your horse.
- Pen and paper
- Leather thong (for mending tack and tying things)
- Fire extinguisher
- Paper towels, wet wipes
- Flashlight (with spare batteries and bulb)
- Trash bags
- Folding chairs
- Waterproof matches (first-aid kit is a good place to store them)
- Manure rake
- Camera

FIRST-AID KIT

From *Mountaineering First Aid*, first aid is defined as "the immediate care given to a person who has been injured or suddenly taken ill." This means first aid must be started in a relatively short time, even though evacuation may be delayed. This includes not only care of physical injuries and protection from the environment, but also care for the victim's mental well-being.

Unless you are dealing with severe, unstoppable blood loss, poisonous bites (snake, spider, scorpion), severe allergic reaction (bee sting), or heart attack, most accidents are not immediately life-threatening. Your goal in giving first aid is to stabilize the patient (horse or human) for transport to a medical facility. With this in mind, we suggest the following first-aid kit:

- Emergency first-aid book for both horse and human. **Read and re-read these books ahead of time. First aid requires a cool head and a plan of action.**
- 3 rolls of Vetrap or other cohesive flexible bandage
- 2 rolls of 4-inch-wide Elastikon or other flexible adhesive bandaging tape
- 3–6 individually wrapped unscented, unpowdered sanitary napkins (absorbent wound dressing)
- 3 rolls brown gauze
- Safety pins
- Pen and paper
- Scissors
- Duct tape
- Easyboot
- Hydrogen peroxide and/or Betadine solution
- 1 extra-large syringe (for irrigating wounds)
- Coins for pay telephone
- Hemostat
- Snake bite antivenin and/or Sawyer Extractor. (Contact your doctor and veterinarian for recommendation.)

- 2 pieces of rubber hosing 3 to 4 inches long (to keep nostrils from swelling shut in case of snake bite)
- Thermometer. If you purchase plastic sheaths, you can use the same thermometer for both horse and human.
- 2–3 rolls of 4-inch-wide bandaging gauze
- Sterile adhesive bandages 1 by 3 inches and other assorted sizes (at least six bandages)
- 10 sterile butterfly closures, small and large
- Tweezers
- Alcohol prep swabs
- Instant cold pack
- Disposable cloths such as Handi Wipes
- Eye wash
- 2 tubes noncortisone eye ointment
- 10 4-by-4-inch sterile gauze pads
- Antiseptic/antibiotic cream, lotion, or liquid
- Compact emergency blanket
- Moleskin and Molefoam
- Antihistamines for human
- Dipyrone (for spasmodic colic, muscular strain)
- Banamine paste (for muscle disorders, lameness, or colic)
- 1 bottle dexamethosone (for allergic reactions, swelling, and fever)
- 1 small bottle acepromazine (tranquilizer)
- Assorted needles and syringes
- Phenylbutazone paste or tablets (for muscle inflammation and lameness)
- Human pain reliever such as aspirin

ON-THE-ROAD SOURCES
FOR LOCAL VETERINARIANS

"The Equine Connection" sponsored by the American Association of Equine Practitioners is a database of member veterinarians. If you are riding during the week and need an emergency veterinarian, give them a call at (800) 438-2386. The line is staffed Monday through Friday 8:00 A.M. to 6:00 P.M. and Saturday 10 A.M. to 2 P.M., central time.

The *North American Horse Travel Guide* lists veterinarians and farriers across the United States and Canada. To order a copy, call (800) 366-0600, or write Roundup Press, P.O. Box 109, Boulder CO 80306-0109.

GENERAL INFORMATION SOURCES

American Horse Council
1700 K Street NW
Washington DC 20006
(202) 296-4031

AVTREC
(Antelope Valley Trails, Recreation,
and Environmental Council)
Elaine Macdonald, President
P.O. Box 3580
Quartz Hill CA 93536-0580
(805) 946-1976

**Backcountry Horsemen of
California, Inc.**
P.O. Box 520
Springville CA 93265
(209) 539-3394

**California Desert Information
Center**
831 Barstow Road
Barstow CA 92311
(619) 255-8760
Monday through Sunday
9 A.M. to 5 P.M.
(The 619 area code will change
to 760 on March 22, 1997.)

**California Recreational Trails
Committee**
(Co-sponsor of the California Trails
Conference)
California Department of Parks
and Recreation
Planning, Acquisition, and Local
Services Division
P.O. Box 942896
Sacramento CA 94296-0001
(916) 653-8615

**California State Horsemen's
Association**
325 B Pollasky Avenue
Clovis CA 93612
(209) 325-1055
Fax (209) 325-1056

**California Trails and Greenways
Foundation**
(Co-sponsor of the California Trails
Conference)
P.O. Box 183
Los Altos CA 94023
(415) 948-1829
Fax (415) 948-1437

**DESTINET State and National
Park Reservation System**
9450 Carroll Park Drive
San Diego CA 92121
(800) 365-2267
8 A.M. to 5 P.M. daily

Equestrian Trails, Inc.
13741 Foothill Blvd. #220
Sylmar CA 91342
(818) 362-6819

Equine Plant Poisoning
National Animal Poison Control
Center
University of Illinois
College of Veterinary Medicine
2001 S. Lincoln Avenue
Urbana IL 61801
(800) 548-2423
$30 per case evaluation

Equine Plant Poisoning (cont.)
Veterinary Practice Publishing
Company
    P.O. Box 4458
    Santa Barbara CA 93140
    (805) 965-1028
    Ask for the *Emergency
    Procedures for Equine
    Toxicoses* chart.

**National Forest Reservation
Center**
    P.O. Box 900
    Cumberland MD 21501-0900
    (800) 280-2267
    Monday through Friday 8:30 A.M.
    to 10:30 P.M.
    Saturday and Sunday 11:00 A.M.
    to 7:00 P.M.

NATRC
(North American Trail Ride Confer-
ence)
National Office
    P.O. Box 2136
    Rancho de Taos NM 87557-2136
    (505) 751-4198
Region 2 (California)
    Judy Kuplent
    14063 Lakeside Street
    Sylmar CA 91342-1610
    (818) 367-6832

Protective Head Gear
American Medical Equestrian
Association
    Attn: J.W. Thomas Byrd, MD
    103 Surrey Road
    Waynesville NC 28786
    (704) 456-3392
International Riding Helmets
    205 Industrial Loop
    Staten Island NY 10309
    (800) 435-6380
Lexington Safety Products
    480 Fairman Road
    Lexington KY 40511
    (606) 233-1404

U.S.G.S.
(U.S. Department of the Interior,
U.S. Geological Survey)
    Earth Science Information Center
    345 Middlefield Road, MS-532
    Menlo Park CA 94025-3591
    (415) 329-4309
    fax (415) 329-5130

BIBLIOGRAPHY

American Horse Council. *1994 Horse Industry Directory*. Washington, D.C.: American Horse Council, 1994.

Bowers, Janice Emily. *100 Desert Wildflowers of the Southwest*. Tucson, AZ: Southwest Parks and Monuments Association, 1989.

Douglass, Don, and Delaine Fragnoli, ed. *Mountain Biking Southern California's Best 100 Trails*. Bishop, CA: Fine Edge Productions, 1993.

Equus magazine. Various issues.

Gagnon, Dennis R. *Exploring the Santa Barbara Backcountry*. Santa Cruz, CA: Western Tanager Press, 1981.

Hayes, Karen, D.V.M. *Emergency! The Active Horseman's Book of Emergency Care*. Boonsboro, MD: Half Halt Press, Inc., 1995.

Hogan, Elizabeth L., ed. *Sunset Western Garden Book*. Menlo Park, CA: Lane Publishing Co., 1988.

Lancaster Woman's Club. *Antelope Valley Wildflower Guide*. Lancaster, CA: Saint Raphael Press, 1978.

Lentz, Martha J., Ph.D., R.N., Steven C. Macdonald, M.P.H., E.M.T., and Jan D. Carline, Ph.D. *Mountaineering First Aid: A Guide to Accident Response and First Aid Care*. 3d ed., rev. Seattle, WA: The Mountaineers, 1990.

Life Nature Library. *The Desert*. New York: Time-Life Books, 1962.

Lindsay, Lowell, and Diana Lindsay. *The Anza-Borrego Desert Region: A Guide to the State Park and Adjacent Areas.* Berkeley, CA: Wilderness Press, 1991.

Mc Auley, Milt. *Wildflowers of the Santa Monica Mountains.* Canoga Park, CA: Canyon Publishing Co., 1985.

Parfit, Michael. "California Desert Lands: A Tribute to Sublime Desolation," *National Geographic*, May 1996, 54–79.

Robinson, John W. *San Bernardino Mountain Trails: 100 Hikes in Southern California.* Berkeley, CA: Wilderness Press, 1986.

Robinson, John W. *Trails of the Angeles: 100 Hikes in the San Gabriels.* Berkeley, CA: Wilderness Press, 1993.

Schaffer, Jeffrey P., Ben Schifrin, Thomas Winnett, and Ruby Johnson Jenkins. *The Pacific Crest Trail Volume I: California.* Berkeley, CA: Wilderness Press, 1995.

Sharp, Robert P., and Allen Glazner. *Geology Underfoot in Southern California.* Missoula, MT: Mountain Press Publishing Company, 1993.

Southern & Central California Atlas & Gazetteer. Freeport, ME: DeLorme Mapping, 1990.

Western Horseman magazine. Various issues.

Williamson, Joseph F., ed. *Sunset Western Garden Book.* Menlo Park, CA: Lane Publishing Company, 1995.

York, Dr. Ben, and Adeline York. *PCT by 2 in 1992.* California, 1992. Duplicated.

INDEX

Crown Valley Press
P.O. Box 336 ◆ Acton CA 93510-0336
(805) 269-1525

To order additional copies of
Horseback Riding Trails of Southern California
use this form (or a facsimile):

	Quantity	Amount
Horseback Riding Trails of Southern California, **Volume I** $14.95	_____	$ _____
Horseback Riding Trails of Southern California, **Volume II** $16.95	_____	$ _____
Horseback Riding Trails of Southern California, **Volume III** (avail. spring 1998, call for price)	_____	$ _____

Subtotal -- $ _____

Tax 8.25% -- $ _____

Handling/Shipping (add $4.50 for the first book,
$2.50 for each additional book) ----------------------- $ _____

TOTAL --- $ _____

Prices subject to change. Allow 2 weeks for delivery.
Please include a check or money order for the total.

Thank You For Your Order!